Lenin on the Question of Nationality

Lenin on the Question of Nationality

by Alfred D. Low

Youngstown University

BOOKMAN ASSOCIATES
New York

TO ROSE, SUZANNE, AND RUTH

"From the point of view of socialism, it is absolutely a
mistake to ignore the tasks of national liberation in
a situation of national oppression."

—V. I. Lenin

"The study of reality was for Lenin only a theoretical
reconnoitre in the interests of action."

—L. Trotsky

"One felt that for the author [Lenin] Marxism was
not an absolute doctrine but a weapon in the revolutionary struggle."

—P. Axelrod

Table of Contents

Introduction

This work is an attempt to analyze and evaluate Lenin's writings on the nationality question—the question primarily of the relation of the dominant Great Russian people to the numerous other nationalities in Russia. These writings date from 1894, the year he published the first book touching on this problem,[1] to the February Revolution. Lenin discusses in the pertinent, largely polemical, essays and articles of this period the basic conceptions of his and the Bolsheviks' nationality policy which are tied together in the slogan of the right of national self-determination.

The most important of Lenin's essays on the nationality question, measured both quantitatively and qualitatively, fall into the period from about 1913 to the February Revolution.[2] While Lenin, prior to 1913, had occasionally written one or the other brief article on selected aspects of the national problem and had some definite views on them, one can hardly speak of Lenin's having a doctrine of nationality or a nationality policy before this time. Most of what he had to say on this question prior to 1913 was limited to the problem of Party organization, a problem which was foremost in the intra-Party disputes of those days. His interest was then focused on the organizational implications of national-cultural autonomy, a concept expounded by the Austrian socialists Rudolf Springer (Karl Renner) and Otto Bauer. It was not until the year 1913 that Lenin began to give fuller consideration to the problem of nationality and its importance for the proletarian and socialist movement.[3]

Did Lenin's thought on the nationality question undergo any change prior to 1917? There is little evidence of it in his writings. If Lenin after 1913 returned to a discussion of some

9

aspect of the nationality problem he had already dealt with before, as, for instance, Party organization and national-cultural autonomy, he had little to add to the previous analysis and re-affirmed the already familiar position. To a large degree, how-ever, he turned his attention to new sides of the complex nationality problem. He did not then abandon his earlier ideas either, but rather developed them. Nor did he change any basic conceptions during the period from 1913 to the February Revolution during which he wrote and published his more im-portant essays on the nationality question. There is, on the whole, a rather striking continuity in his thought on this problem up to the Revolution, and even beyond it.

The tense international situation on the eve of World War I and the beginning of hostilities placed the problem of nationality in the foreground. This was a period during which territorial questions in general, in Europe and in the colonies, received considerable attention, and the attitude of Russia's numerous border nationalities in particular acquired, according to Lenin, "special urgency." [4] The role of these national minorities dur-ing the war and the problems of war aims and future boundaries occupied many minds, including those of leading statesmen, of the Russians, of their allies and of their foes, of bourgeois capitalists and of socialists of all shades and persuasions. The question of nationality became again the object of a prolonged debate within the Party,[5] revealing wide differences concerning tactics and goals. Lenin himself was then especially concerned about the relation between the fighting proletariat and the na-tional liberation movement during the stages prior to the "pro-letarian" revolution. By 1917 Lenin's thought on the nationality question had already attained definite shape, and the Bolshevik nationality program was completed.[6]

In 1913 Stalin too had turned to the discussion of the ques-tion of nationality. At the suggestion, and under the guidance, of Lenin, Stalin wrote the essay *Marxism and the National Ques-tion*,[7] which is considered by many his most significant contribution to Bolshevik theoretical literature. There can be little doubt about the role in the realm at first of theory and then of practice which Stalin has played in shaping the national policy of the Soviet Union.[8] A comparison, however, of Lenin's and Stalin's writings on the problem of nationality prior to 1917 clearly reveals Stalin's dependence on Lenin. Even in this limited field, the national question—which was Stalin's specialty—Lenin was the guiding hand and the more important and more original thinker.[9]

The author has found it best to organize the material in accordance with the Marxist conception of the principal stages of economic, social, and political development of man, the concept which also underlies Lenin's political thought. Lenin has repeatedly pointed out that the Party's nationality policy was contingent upon the particular stage of development of the respective nationalities and states.[10] He did not, however, give all stages equal attention. A "practical" politician, Lenin was in regard to the nationality question most concerned with the present and the immediate future rather than with the past and the distant future. The organization of this study necessarily reflects to some degree Lenin's more detailed discussion of Bolshevik nationality policy in some stages and his cursory treatment of other periods.

Since Lenin's thought in the realm of nationalism and nationality policy was, as mentioned, fully developed by 1917 and had been expressed prior to that time, this study has in general been limited to the period up to the February Revolution. Lenin, however, did not swerve from the main course of his "doctrine" of nationality after the seizure of power. E. H. Carr emphasizes on one occasion[11] that the experience of power brought no radical change in Lenin's philosophy of the state. The same may be said of his thought on nationality.

Lenin's thought on the nationality question underwent some modifications after the November Revolution, yet on the whole it was rather a shift of emphasis than an outright change. Prior to 1917 Lenin wrote in the capacity of theoretician and tactician. Thereafter, he faced the urgent practical problems of the statesman and of the administrator. Yet even when Lenin seemed to reverse himself, as in matters of federalism, the groundwork for the "change" was actually laid in the prerevolutionary period.

This study is confined to a segment only, though an important one, of Lenin's political thought. It is not a study of Soviet nationality policy; yet it is to a degree related to it, since Lenin's ideas on nationality have largely shaped Soviet policy and made their imprint upon the life of the nationalities of the Soviet Union. Lenin's widow, Madame N. K. Krupskaya, stressed this very point in her *Memories of Lenin* when she wrote:

> The controversy [on the nationality question in 1913] proved to be very useful, for it helped our party to solve the national problem in the Soviet state when it was established.[12]

An attempt has been made in this study to indicate which elements of Lenin's thought on nationality have been woven into the fabric of the U. S. S. R., and in what manner.

Is Lenin's thought on nationality of current significance? Since the death of Stalin and, in particular, since Krushchev's sensational speech denouncing Stalin at the Twentieth Congress of the Communist Party of the U. S. S. R in February, 1956, Leninism, Lenin's teaching on the policies and on the tactics and strategy of the proletariat and of the Soviet Union, has had a striking renascence. The posthumous dethronement of Stalin, his relegation to a position of lesser importance, enhances, of course, the contemporary import of Lenin's thought and, in particular, its importance in relation to the nationality question.

Lenin's ideas on nationality were developed with the view to the proletariat's exploiting the grievances of oppressed nationalities, primarily in Russia, but also in other multinational states and colonial empires. His nationality program, as well as all other aspects of his political and social thought, though born of Russian conditions and especially geared to Russia, had always general significance and universal applicability. Since the communists hold that Lenin's teachings, including those on the nationality question, offer the precept for the seizure of power everywhere, it is self-evident why the free world should acquaint itself with the pertinent body of Lenin's thought.

Lenin stressed that the nationality policy of the Bolshevik Party must be based upon real equality between nationalities. Real national equality, however, was not achieved by the Party, not even during Lenin's lifetime, in spite of claims to the contrary. The October Revolution had been primarily the accomplishment of the Great Russian proletariat, and the "working class" of the Great Russian nation retained and increasingly strengthened its position in the Stalinist era. During and after World War II, Stalin, the "assimilated Great-Russian," [13] extolled the Great Russian nationality as the first and "leading force among all the peoples of our country." [14] The pretense of equality of Russia's many different nationalities was thus abandoned.

Just as there is no real equality among the nationalities of the U. S. S. R., there also is no genuine equality in the relations between either the U. S. S. R. and communist-dominated states in Eastern Europe or between the Communist Party of the Soviet Union and the communist parties of the rest of the world. From their inception the relations of the U. S. S. R. and her Communist Party to virtually all other communist-governed states and their communist parties were those of master and servant, and the former denied to the latter genuine equality and independence.

Russian nationalist intransigence and Soviet imperialism have eventually produced 'Titoism,' 'national communism,' first in Yugoslavia and then in the rest of the Soviet satellite empire, and, more recently, have brought about revolutions in Hungary and Poland. These uprisings have shaken the Soviet Empire and bared the true character of the hold of the U. S. S. R. on her East-European neighbors.

Lenin, primarily concerned with developing the Party's nationality policy for the purpose of facilitating the "proletarian" seizure of power and then perpetuating it, insisted upon the program of full national equality in the multinational state in the bourgeois-capitalist era and in the stages of the proletarian revolution and proletarian dictatorship. It was the polyglot state and the proletariat's policy in regard to the nationality problem which became the focus of his attention. While he had little to say about the relationship of the victorious working classes of two neighboring proletarian states—an international problem rather than an intra-national one, and one of the most pressing for the Soviets in the post-war era—it is clear that, in the spirit of his pronouncements on the nationality question, equality was to mark not only the relations between the different nationalities of the same state, but was also to prevail between different sovereign "proletarian" states and nationalities. In the Stalinist era, however, and again after the recent Hungarian revolution, the Soviet leaders strongly emphasized the importance of the leadership of the Communist Party of the Soviet Union—the older experienced brother—among the communist parties of the world, and justified Russian claims to preeminence in the communist orbit.

Lenin's unceasing, though even in his lifetime not effective, insistence on national equality has not been heeded in the Soviet Union, neither in its internal policy nor in its external one. Nor is it likely that the rebirth of Leninism, the greater stress on Lenin's thought during the last years, will by itself produce a change for the better. After all, mere lip-service to Lenin had been paid even in the Stalinist era. And the present rulers of the Soviet Union are likely to give to Lenin's thought and to his not always consistent utterances such interpretation as the hour demands. In addition, their repression of the Hungarian revolution was in the best Stalinist tradition, and after a period of relaxation of some controls, internally and externally, also in regard to their East European satellites, they have again tightened the screws in conformity with the Stalinist pattern.

Yet many communists, in Eastern Europe and elsewhere, may be relied upon to justify in the future their demands for national equality, independence, and brotherly "proletarian" attitudes by reference to Lenin, and in particular to his body of thought on the nationality question. In his address to the Central Committee of the Polish United Workers Party on October 20, 1956, Wladyslaw Gomulka stressed the importance of the "renascence of Leninist principles in the labor movement" against "alien excrescences and distortions in theory and practice." [15]

A detailed analysis of Lenin's thought on nationality does lend no strength either to Stalinism and its claim to preeminence of the Great Russians in the U. S. S. R. as well as throughout the entire communist world, or to those dedicated to the concept of genuine equality in the proletarian multinational realm and among the different sovereign socialist national states.

In his thought on nationality, Lenin, contrary to superficial appearances, was partial to the Great Russian people and other large nationalities and considered the smaller nationalities expendable and their rights to self-determination not absolutely valid. This position, however, was not clearly and openly proclaimed, but for obvious reasons rather shrouded in ambiguities. Nowhere in his pertinent writings did Lenin go so far as to justify the use of "proletarian" force against other nationalities, whether living inside of Russia or outside of it. In theory Lenin rejected such means, though not on ethical, but rather on tactical and political grounds.

The growing trend toward nationalism, apparent in the Soviet Union for many years, also fits ill with Lenin's professions of internationalism and espousal even of cosmopolitanism. After World War II Stalinist Russia went to the most baffling extremes of nationalism, cultural isolationism, and deprecation of foreign cultures. Cosmopolitanism became a word of reproach and was held to be diametrically opposed to Soviet patriotism. It became linked with imperialism and Zionism— one of the newer "evils"—with rootlessness and spineless imitation of foreign cultures; in short, it became a byword of shame, treason, and disgrace. Even as rigid an adherent of historical dialetics as he was, Lenin could not have foreseen how far the historic pendulum would swing away from the early internationalism into the opposite direction, a direction virtually indistinguishable from that of the most rabid and chauvinistic fascism.

Much as cosmopolitanism has been denounced in the U. S. S. R. during the last decade, there can be no doubt that Lenin's writings on the nationality problem establish him as a convinced cosmopolite, who considered "fusion," "merger" and "amalgamation" of nationalities, in short extinction of many of them, as hopeful and promising tendencies. Of course, he may have suspected that in the process of assimilation the larger and more numerous nationalities, including the Great Russian people, were likely to have an edge over the smaller- and middle-sized nationalities. While the latter would be submerged, the former would survive and emerge only slightly modified in ethnic composition, character, and outlook.

On the whole, nationalism, even though progressive, was for Lenin never an end in itself and had for him no value as such. He looked upon the national liberation movement as a mere instrument which, if skilfully used, might speed the "proletarian" seizure of power.

During and since World War II the U. S. S. R. and world communism have scored tremendous gains. The Soviet Union, annexing new territories and enclosing additional non-Great-Russian peoples as well as imposing domination upon her smaller neighbors, has become a new colonial and imperialistic power of vast dimensions. At the same time the U. S. S. R. has dared to pose as champion of the nations either still ruled by Western imperialist powers or until recently governed by them and continues to woo them. In view of these developments, Lenin's point of view in regard to nationality and national culture and his claim of holding in his hand the solution to the vexing nationalities problem holds special contemporary significance.

The new Soviet colonialism and imperialism is the sharpest contradiction to Lenin's continually stressed policy of national equality and self-determination. It is clearly irreconcilable with his professed nationality policy.

Soviet propaganda ought to be deflated not only by contrasting Lenin's professed policy with Soviet reality concerning the nationalities, but also by a closer analysis of Lenin's thought on the nationality problem. By revealing the numerous contradictions and inconsistencies in Lenin's thought and disclosing especially the Great Russian bias embedded in it, the hopes and expectations the downtrodden peoples have placed on the saving power of world communism and of the U. S. S. R. ought to be shattered. Such an analysis should drive home to the oppressed peoples of the world as well as to those who have acquired political freedom only recently that they were little appreciated by Lenin for their own sake, but were rather considered by him to be pawns in the game of proletarian and international power politics, to be used today and discarded to-morrow.

The edition of Lenin's *Sochineniia* used throughout this work is the second edition, though other editions have been consulted too. The very few quotations from Lenin's works not made from the second edition of *Sochineniia* have been properly marked. Beginning with the year 1918, the dates used are those of the Gregorian Calendar.

The author, an Austrian by birth, has been interested in the nationality problem in general, in that of Austria with its multinational past in particular, and in the theoretical discussions of the nationality question by socialist and Marxist writers since his student days at the University of Vienna. Research for this work was undertaken in 1953-54 while he studied under a Faculty Fellowship from the Fund for the Advancement of Education at The Russian Institute of Columbia University. The author is greatly indebted to the Fund for having enabled him to engage in research in the Russian area. Of course, the Fund bears no responsibility for the conclusions which he has reached and which have been presented in this study.

The same applies to the following persons who have kindly given of their time to examine the manuscript and have been most helpful in various ways. The writer wishes to acknowledge his debt to Professor Geroid T. Robinson of The Russian Institute of Columbia University for his penetrating analysis of the manuscript and his valuable suggestions. He is also grateful to Dr. Philip E. Mosely for the assistance given him in the field of Russian Studies in general, and to Dr. Harold L. Dean, Dr. Robert J. Taylor, and Professors Morris Slavin and Alvin Skardon for having read the manuscript in its entirety. Last but not least, he is greatly indebted to his wife, Dr. Rose S. Low, for her steady encouragement and critical examination of this study.

ALFRED D. LOW

Youngstown, Ohio,
January, 1958.

CHAPTER ONE

Russian Socialism and the Nationality Problem Under Tsarism

When the Bolsheviks seized power in Russia in October, 1917, they inherited a multinational state beset by numerous problems of which the problem of nationality was not the least important one. The census of the year 1897 had disclosed that non-Great-Russians constituted the majority of the population of the Tsarist Empire, about 56% of its inhabitants. During the First World War they supplied as many as 45% of Russia's soldiers.

The Great Russian people, living in the interior of the Empire, formed its historic core. In the course of centuries the Russian state had pushed its frontiers forward until it embraced and dominated millions of non-Russian nationalities which populated the peripheral regions of the Empire. In the twentieth century an increasing number of them demanded autonomy, but did not wish separation from the polyglot state. Strategically located outposts of Great Russian settlers, especially in the towns and cities of the outlying regions, constituted a centripetal and integrating influence in the Empire. Some of the "alien" peoples, like the Poles, the Finns, the Germans, the Armenians, and the Georgians, were the bearers of a high civilization, of rich cultural and national traditions, and were also economically advanced, while others, like the Mongolians, many of the Caucasian peoples, and numerous smaller ethnic units, especially in Asia, were culturally inferior to the Great Russians and economically backward.

19

Some of the western appendages of Tsarist Russia, such as Poland between 1815 and 1831 and Finland throughout the nineteenth century, enjoyed at times a large degree of autonomy under special "Constitutions." But the Russian autocracy often withdrew arbitrarily concessions granted earlier or violated even contractual agreements.

In the Baltic provinces and in Poland the difference of nationality was, as elsewhere in Russia, aggravated by social and economic cleavages and by religious diversity. In the Baltic region the upper class was German and Lutheran, while the lower classes were Esthonian and Lettish and, by religion, Uniate* or Orthodox. The Baltic Germans, forming the economic and cultural backbone of the area, played a most important role in the administration of the Russian Empire and loyally supported the Russian autocracy.

In Russian Poland the ruling class was Polish and Catholic, the lower classes, however, were White Russian and Ukrainian, and, religiously, Uniate and Orthodox. Industrialization had proceeded here in the late nineteenth and early twentieth century at a more rapid pace than in Russia herself, and had sharpened the resistance to Russian autocracy on both social-revolutionary and national grounds, though the nationalist Polish bourgeoisie under the leadership of Roman Dmowski did not press for separation and a portion of the Polish proletariat, led by Rosa Luxemburg, also opposed secession.

Both the Ukraine and White Russia were likewise ethnically very mixed regions. Centuries of political separation, during which Ukrainians and White Russians had been subjected to Polish-Lithuanian domination, had left their mark upon them and had created a gulf separating them from the Great Russians. The Ukrainians, according to the census of 1897 more than twenty-two million people, were predominantly rural, while the cities and towns in their midst were largely

---

* A Christian of an Eastern rite who acknowledged the Pope's primacy.

inhabited by Great Russians, Poles, and Jews. These same elements and Lithuanians and White Russians lived in Lithuania and White Russia, which were administratively linked. White Russians at the turn of the century numbered almost six million. While Poles and Jews monopolized trade and industry in these areas and Great Russians and Lithuanians owned landed estates, the White Russians were impoverished peasants, socially and economically exploited, and politically and religiously oppressed.

The Jews, more scattered than any other people in Russia, resided primarily in the western provinces and in the Ukraine. Subject to special legislation, they were one of the most persecuted of all nationalities of Russia. Separated by religion, language, and occupation from the other ethnic and religious groups, the tsarist autocracy found in the Jews an ideal scapegoat for diverting the wrath of the Great Russian nation and of the subject peoples from itself and the real causes of their misery.

Especially variegated was the national, religious, and racial picture in the Caucasian region. There, in addition to about four million Great Russians, Ukrainians and White Russians, lived during the First World War 1,860,000 Armenians, an approximately equal number of Georgians, about 2,500,000 Azerbaijanis and other Moslems, and a bewildering array of other mountain peoples. While the Georgians had a rather small and little influential middle class, this element was dominant among the Armenians; the latter were deeply aroused by the massacres of their people in the neighboring Ottoman Empire. Numerous small minorities lived among the Christian Georgians and Armenians as well as among the Moslem Azerbaijanis.

At the turn of the century there were altogether almost fourteen million Turkic peoples in the Russian Empire. Though linguistically closely related among each other and linked by common ancestry and Islamic religion, no political pan-Turkic movement arose among them to address the widely scattered groups. Islam and the Islamic way of life rather than well-developed ethnic consciousness or feeling established common ties among them. Culturally and economically the most advanced of all Turkic peoples were the Volga Tatars who included urban middle-class elements. In regard to their general development they were followed by the Crimean Tatars and the Azerbaijanis of Transcaucasia, the Uzbeks, the Turkmens, the Kirghiz and the Kazaks of Central Asia, the Bashkirs of the Ural region, and numerous other predominantly agricultural and pastoral peoples and tribes of Siberia.

Beginning with the regime of Tsar Alexander III, a policy of intensive Russification, closely linked with one which favored the Greek-Orthodox Church and sharply discriminated against non-orthodox religious groups, drove the numerous nationalities into bitter opposition to the regime and made them receptive to revolutionary propaganda. The growing discrimination against non-Great-Russian nationalities was grist upon the mill of revolutionary movements. It focused their attention upon untapped revolutionary potentialities and induced them to take a stand for national equality and for national rights. The revolution of 1905 again underlined the importance of the nationality problem. Russian socialists of all shades gave their attention not only to the class struggle, but also to national and religious oppression and adopted some nationality program.

Socialism and nationalism, two of the most powerful ideologies and movements of today, are of comparatively recent origin. Both products of the industrial age, they developed side by side in nineteenth-century Europe, often in sharp rivalry with each other, only late to reach in some countries an uneasy understanding between themselves. The relationship between socialism and nationalism attained special urgency in multinational states, such as Austria and Russia, where it posed a serious and baffling problem for the socialist parties.

It was in Austria that socialism began to take realistic account of the complex problem of nationality and of national movements. A most important discusssion of the nationality question took place at the Bruenn Congress of the Austrian Social Democratic Party which was held in 1899. One of the solutions then proposed was to divide the Austro-Hungarian Dual Empire into ethnically more or less homogeneous provinces and to grant them jurisdiction in cultural and linguistic matters. This proposal rested on the principle of territorial national-cultural autonomy.[1]

Another plan, suggested at that time, provided for extraterritorial national-cultural autonomy. This proposal was based upon granting to every nationality autonomy in cultural and linguistic matters. It offered national autonomy, the guarantee of national preservation, to minorities which were geographically surrounded by members of another national group—as, for instance, the Czechs in Vienna, the German Saxons in Transylvania, and the German Swabians in the Banat—and also to other national minorities in the various Austrian crownlands, the members of which lived dispersed throughout the Austrian Empire rather than compactly settled.

The Bruenn Congress, adopting a program which represented a compromise between the two foregoing proposals, emphasized that Austria must be transformed into a democratic federation of nationalities and rejected any "national privilege," including a state language.[2]

In the following decade the Austrian socialists Karl Renner and Otto Bauer developed in their pioneering works on the nationality problem more fully the concept of extraterritorial national-cultural autonomy which was centered on the individual[3] rather than on territory and which gave the scattered nationalities about as extensive cultural and linguistic rights as those nations which were compactly settled. These writers, facing in Austria's polyglot empire vast national problems which threatened not only to disrupt the state but also to weaken

international proletarian solidarity and to thwart socialist agitation, were the first in the camp of international socialism to
come theoretically to grips with the phenomenon of nationality,
largely overlooked by Marx and Engels themselves. They also
made practical recommendations for a solution of the national
differences which plagued the Austrian state. Their program
was designed to save the Austrian Empire and at the same time
to remove a most serious obstacle in the path of Austrian
socialism.[4]

The Austrian socialists' analysis of the national problem as
well as their recommendations for the solution of the national
question made a great impression upon large sections of Russian
socialists. They quickly began making applications to Russia
and took positions either pro or contra the main Austrian lines
of thought. The Jewish *Bund,* the White Russian Socialist
Hromada, the Georgian Socialist Federalist Party *Sakartvelo,*
the Armenian *Dashnakstutiun,*[5] and other socialists became convinced proponents of the Austrian socialists' doctrine of extraterritorial national-cultural autonomy.

Of these groups, the Bund (All-Jewish Workers' Union in
Russia and Poland), representing a good section of the working
class of the Jewish people which lived more dispersed throughout Russia than any other nationality, embraced wholeheartedly
the concept of extraterritorial national-cultural autonomy. The
Austrian plan, designed to solve the vexing national problem
in the heart of Central Europe, seemed to the Bund an equally
ingenious device for the solution of the problem of nationality
in the Russian multinational realm.

The Bund, formed in Vilna in 1897, joined the new Russian
Social Democratic Labor Party the following year; it was to
be independent only in such questions which related exclusively
to the Jewish proletariat. Having first demanded merely legal
equality for the Jews, the Bund at its Fourth Congress in 1901
asserted its claim to a national status for the Jewish people
and to extraterritorial national-cultural autonomy. Since the

Bund's concept of the future Russia was that of a state based upon a "federation of nationalities," the Bund correspondingly asked also for a federalization of the Russian Social Democratic Labor Party at the latter's Second Congress held in 1903. When the Party rejected these demands, the Bund withdrew in protest, severing its ties with it. It was not until 1906 at the Fourth Congress of the R. S. D. R. P. in Stockholm, the so-called "Unification Congress," that the Bund, and also the Social Democrats of Poland, Lithuania, and Latvia, rejoined the Party as regional organizations.[6]

In readmitting the Bund, the Party avoided taking a position in regard to national-cultural autonomy which the former had only recently reasserted, at its Fourth Conference in 1905. Real clarification of the national program was thus not achieved within the ranks of the Party, just as other major theoretical differences were not settled in this pre-war period. The nationality question remained therefore among Russian Social Democrats a controversial subject prior to World War I, assuming major importance with the year 1913. The dispute, created by the demands of some for national-cultural autonomy and federalization of the Party, was, however, by no means the only issue which divided Social Democrats in respect to the national question. A good many, including the most prominent Party members, maintained serious reservations about the Party's nationality program, the right to national self-determination, meaning to secession, and some questioned it outright.

Three lines of thought emerged thus in the early twentieth century in the course of the prolonged and often bitter debates of Russian socialists on the question of nationality. We shall refer to the three positions taken as those of the Right, the Left and the Center.[7] The position of the Right was that of the Bund, of many socialists of other national minorities, and of all others supporting extraterritorial national-cultural autonomy and also federalization of the Party. The Left was formed by those internationalists who were unwilling to make any concession to nationalism and rejected national self-determination as the program of the Party. Its leading spokesmen were Rosa Luxemburg,[8] Nikolai Bukharin, Karl Radek and Grigorii Piatakov. The Center was the position taken by Lenin himself who pleaded for recognition of the reality of nationalism. He demanded support for the Party program of the right to national self-determination, meaning to secession, which, he claimed, would further the proletarian class struggle rather than divert from it. The dispute among these different groups in the Party centered thus on national self-determination and its interpretation; the leftist, internationalist wing of the Party simply tended to disregard the Party's national program, while both the Right and Lenin upheld the right to self-determination, though they sharply differed in their interpretations of it.[9]

While the Left followed Marx and Engels in their tendency partly of minimizing the nationality question and partly of suspecting[10] nationalism, the Right turned in its analysis of the nationality problem and in subsequent recommendations concerning nationality policy to the Austrian socialists Karl Renner and Otto Bauer. Lenin himself referred to the masters though, in his own words, rather to the spirit of Marx and Engels than to their letter;[11] he pointed, not without reason, to the vast changes in historical conditions which had occurred since their death and to the increased importance of nationalism in Europe and the world.

Lenin's theory of national self-determination was, according to his own account, based not only upon the position of Marx and Engels, but also upon the stand taken by the Second International at its London Congress in July and August, 1896. The Congress had proclaimed the "full right of self-determination of all nations." [12] Lenin had then no issue with the analysis of the nationality question and policy recommendation of the Second International, just as, prior to World War I, he did not question but approved a good number of other views and policies of the Second International.[13]

The First Congress of the Russian Social Democratic Labor Party was held in 1898, two years after the London Congress of the International. While the latter had adopted the program of national self-determination, the RSDLP made in its initial manifesto no reference to self-determination.[14] The Second Party Congress in 1903, however, embodied the right to self-determination in point 9 of its program.[15] This program was repeatedly confirmed in the following decade.

Lenin's move into Austrian Poland in 1912 made him more keenly aware of the urgency of the problem of nationality and of the international implications of the Party slogan of the right to national self-determination. In the summer of 1913 the Party's Central Committee interpreted the right to self-determination as "the right to secession and formation of an independent state." [16] Lenin himself saw little difference between the Bolshevik position taken at this Conference—which was his own[17]—and the declaration of the London Congress of the Second International.[18]

Did Lenin interpret the International's demand for national self-determination correctly when he identified it with the right to secession? The International's demand did not exclude the possibility of secession, but was not identical with it; it could be interpreted as including the right to federalism, to autonomy, to national-cultural autonomy, etc. The Austrian socialists' position as well as that of the Bund, of the entire Russian Right on the nationality question, was much closer to the spirit of the Second International than the position of Lenin himself.

CHAPTER TWO

Lenin on the Transient Character
of Nationalism

LENIN'S NEGATIVISM

Nationalism was looked upon by Lenin as a temporary phenomenon. It was to him a by-product of the historical evolution of capitalism.[1] Owing its origin to it, nationalism was also doomed to die with it. This conviction of the merely transient character of the movement of nationalism colored Lenin's entire thinking about the nationality problem.

Lenin neither approved nor disapproved of the national movement and of its objective, the independent national state. He recognized the reality of national feeling and potency of national endeavors and was impressed by the strength of some national movements. His major, his only, concern was the class struggle and the preparation for the "proletarian" seizure of power. His sense for tactical opportunities made him look upon the national liberation movement as a potential ally[2] of the proletariat of the dominant and imperialist nations.

But he also looked upon nationalism as a possible rival to socialism. He feared its appeal to the proletariat; he excoriated national culture and pleaded for international culture[3] and assimilation. A potential temporary ally of the proletariat, nationalism was also likely to be dangerous to it, to undermine the workers' solidarity, to become a weapon in the hands of the bourgeoisie and of Tsarism. It was a two-edged sword and had to be carefully wielded.

The national movement of the oppressed nationalities was for Lenin a convenient political tool,[4] never an end in itself.

28

He was willing to use the instrument as long as it appeared to be serviceable, but resolved to discard it when its possible harm threatened to exceed its benefits. Nationality had for him only an instrumental value. He did not discern any worth in it, but saw in it only a help and sometimes a hindrance. There was a streak of coolness, of indifference, toward the national movement in Lenin's thought. He did not waste any love on it.

Neither does Lenin waste time defining, characterizing, and explaining the phenomena of nationality and of nationalism. One will look in vain in his pertinent writings for a definition of nationality, for an exposition of its essence and character.[5] While he devotes considerable space to a discussion of the Party's nationality policy and of its meaning and writes abundantly on the Party's tactics and strategy in regard to the national problem, he does not come to grips with the more abstract and theoretical, and less urgent and practical, problem of the character and essence of nationality and nationalism.

If one wishes to look for a brief definition of nationality in the contemporary Bolshevik literature, one will have to turn to Stalin's essay on the nationality problem, "Marxism and the National Question," which was written in 1913 at Lenin's instigation and under his guidance. On the whole, Lenin's and Stalin's views on the nationality problem, as expressed in the years just prior to the War and during the first years of World War I, were identical, though there were a number of revealing minor differences.[6] It is most likely that Stalin's definition of nationality was on the whole acceptable to Lenin.

Stalin, in an unoriginal manner, defined nationality as a historically evolved group which had a common language and culture[7] and revealed common psychological traits, possessed a territorial base, and was held together by strong economic ties. While Otto Bauer had offered a novel and arresting interpretation of nationality—seeing in it a group tied together by common character traits which resulted from common historical experiences—Stalin reverted from this dynamic to a rather static conception of nationality, to a pedestrian listing of a number of criteria generally found in an ethnic group. Though there was no striking omission or error in Stalin's sketchy definition, it could hardly be looked upon as a distinguished and significant Marxist contribution to the discussion of nationality. It contained little which set it apart from the "bourgeois" theories of nationality, except perhaps the emphasis on its temporary, changing, character. Yet while Stalin made an attempt to define nationality, Lenin, too occupied with immediate, pressing problems of Bolshevik policy, did not even try.

Lenin was less concerned with the essence of nationality and of nationalism and more with the possible alliance between national liberation movements and the fighting proletariat. He wished to develop a propagandistically effective slogan in order to attract the oppressed nationalities to the banner of the Party. Thus he forged the weapon of national self-determination and continued to keep its edges sharp.

Self-determination is presented by Lenin as the real core of his and the Bolsheviks' nationality program. But nationalism and nationality were not valuable as such. Nationalities were given political opportunities, not because they deserved them, not on account of cultural or political creativeness, of promise or accomplishment, but merely because they had suffered oppression in the past, because Tsarism was especially "reactionary" and "barbaric," because the "freedom" of the Great Russian nationality itself and the interests of "democracy" and socialism[8] demanded it. The conception of the right of every nationality to establish a national state of its own hid a strong element of negativism.

Indifferent as Lenin is to the "rights" of the nationality, he is equally indifferent to the goal of the national liberation movement, the national state. Lenin displays complete lack of enthusiasm for nationalities and national states. Both are to him without intrinsic value, and both transient. National culture is for Lenin merely bourgeois culture, and nationalism is merely an inevitable stage, an unavoidable detour on the road to internationalism. Capitalism is a stage which is closer to socialism than feudalism is, but it does not elicit any joy on just this ground. The national state, on the whole, is in some important respects superior to the generally backward multinational state and closer to the ultimate stage of internationalism; but it is still too far from the millennium to arouse any enthusiasm.

The future belongs to internationalism, more specifically to cosmopolitanism, and assimilation is applauded. Cosmopolitanism is unavoidable, the inevitable goal, and fortunately, it is also most desirable.

Lenin should have been able to think in terms of the future, of the phenomenon of nationality cleansed of national hate, jealousy, and chauvinism. Yet he held that under socialism not only national hate, nationalist tensions and struggles were bound to disappear, but also nationalities as such. This superficial view, which was rooted rather in wishful thinking than based on clearly noticeable historic trends, held, however, Lenin and the Bolsheviks captive as well as a good number of other socialists in Russia and elsewhere.

There is an unmistakable ambivalence in Lenin's feeling and thought on nationality. He is cool, indifferent, even hostile to the national state and to nationality. But, in general, the proletariat and the Party have the solemn obligation to support the national liberation movement because democracy and socialism demand it.

What is the explanation for this apparent inconsistency and contradiction in Lenin's position toward nationalism which runs like a red thread throughout his writings on this question?

THE NATIONAL PROBLEM AND ITS HISTORIC SETTING

The problem of nationality, according to Lenin, can be fully comprehended only if it is placed within its historic setting:

The categorical demand of Marxian theory in examining any social question is that it be placed within *definite* historical limits . . . It is impossible to begin drawing up the national program of the Marxists of a given country without taking into account all the . . . general historical and concrete state conditions.[9]

Marx and Engels had always "recognized" the "historical relativity" of the national question.[10]

"Developing capitalism," Lenin elaborates in the essay "Critical Notes on the National Question," shows "two historical tendencies" in regard to nationalism.

The first is the awakening of national life and of national movements, the struggle against all national oppression, the creation of nation states. The second is the development and growing frequency of all sorts of relations between nations, the breaking down of national barriers, the creation of the international unity of capital, and of economic life in general, of politics, of science, and so forth.

Both tendencies are the universal law of capitalism. The first predominates at the beginning of its development, the second characterizes mature capitalism as it approaches its transformation into a socialist society.[11]

The proletariat's and the Party's[12] policy in regard to the nationality question is thus by no means uniform in the period prior to the "proletarian" revolution. There are rather two distinct positions that the Marxist Party must take which correspond to two distinct stages in the development of nationalism under capitalism. In the first stage the Party must "defend . . . the equal rights of nations and languages," the "inadmissibility of any privileges of any kind" and "also the right of nations to self-determination." In the second stage—the dividing line between these two stages being represented by the "bourgeois-democratic revolution" [13]—the Party must uphold, as stated here, the "principle of internationalism." As is made clear, this includes support for the principle of self-determination.

The first stage in the development of nationalism, Lenin elaborated, was climaxed by the establishment of the national state. "The period of the final victory over feudalism" was everywhere in the world "linked with national movements." And the "tendency of every national movement" was the formation of national states. "The requirements of modern capitalism" were "best satisfied" in the framework of the national state. "Economic factors" drove nationalities towards the goal of the national state, "and for the whole of Western Europe, nay, for the entire civilized world, the typical, the normal state for the capitalist period" was "therefore the national state." [14] Judged by the needs of the capitalist order, multinational states, such as for instance Russia and Austria-Hungary, represented less developed types of states.[15]

In most Western countries the nationality question had been solved long ago. No multinational state had survived in the West and no national problem existed. In these countries the nationality question belonged to the past.[16]

In Western continental Europe the period of bourgeois-democratic revolutions embraces a fairly definite period of time, approximately from 1789-1871. It was precisely this epoch that was the epoch of national movements and the creation of national states.[17]

But in most surviving multinational states, as also in Russia, "the bourgeois-democratic reformation" had not been completed, and the national movement was of greatest importance. The same held true of the entire East, of Africa, Asia, and of the colonies, where the national movement was a present problem as well as a future one. Colonial problems were really national ones.[18]

In Eastern Europe and in Asia the period of bourgeois-democratic revolutions started not before 1905. The revolutions in Russia, Persia, Turkey, and China, the wars in the Balkans, such is the chain of world events of *our* period in our 'Orient.' And only the blind can fail to see the awakening of a *whole* series of bourgeois-democratic national movements, strivings to create nationally independent and nationally united states in this chain of events.[19]

In the nineteenth century the struggle for national liberation and independence is a struggle against obsolete feudal and autocratic forces, carried on by the bourgeoisie which has espoused liberalism and political democracy. In the twentieth century, however, nationalism takes the form of a struggle of the national minorities of Eastern Europe against Great Russian and Turkish oppression and of colonial countries for national freedom against the imperialism of the great European powers. Since these powers are internally threatened by the class-conscious socialist proletariat, the national movement, especially in Eastern Europe and in the colonies, becomes a potential ally of the proletariat of the imperialist oppressor nations. It is this possible alliance which arouses Lenin's special interest.

> It is precisely and solely because Russia and the neighboring countries are passing through this epoch [the epoch of the "bourgeois-democratic national movements"] that we require an item in our program on the right of nations to self-determination.[20]

The problem of nationality and national oppression must be met by the proletariat by adopting the slogan of the right to national self-determination, by "consistent" application of "democracy."

An example of a country which had solved its national question was Switzerland. "It is an indubitable and indisputable fact," Lenin writes in rather complimentary fashion in regard to Switzerland, "that the national peace under the rule of capitalism (as far as it is realizable at all) is exclusively to be realized in countries with consistent democracy." [21] Bourgeois democracy, however, is only rarely held to be consistent democracy.

The nationality question will be fully solved only under socialism. The right to self-determination will become universally recognized only after the "proletarian" revolution. In the meantime, self-interest as well as principles will demand that the proletariat raise the banner of self-determination in capitalist states. Yet the proletariat's support of the bourgeois-led emancipation movement will never be unconditional. While generally backing the national liberation movement, the proletariat will never lose sight of socialist interests and of international goals.

Nationality Policy Before the "Proletarian" Revolution

WHAT IS NATIONAL SELF-DETERMINATION?

What was Lenin's conception of self-determination? This term persistently recurs in his writings and forms the backbone of his nationality policy. Lenin elaborated upon it in numerous essays, articles, letters, and Party resolutions. A clear perception of its meaning is essential for an understanding of Lenin's and the Bolsheviks' conception of the national problem. A brief preliminary definition therefore appears in order at this stage.

National self-determination has, according to Lenin, a concrete meaning. It signifies the right of the oppressed nationality to secession. Self-determination and secession are thus equated.[1] The right, however, to secede, is not equivalent to the necessity or desirability of secession. For instance, a democrat and a socialist must demand also full freedom of divorce for the "oppressed sex" "although it is not at all difficult to understand that the recognition of the *right* of women to leave their husbands is not an *invitation* to all wives to do so!"[2] In the great majority of cases the "proletarian" revolution will give the formerly oppressed nationality the first opportunity of demonstrating freely its desires and realizing its wishes. The border nationality will freely decide whether it wishes to depart from the multinational state or whether, in view of the just attained equality and the expectation also of future freedom, it ought to throw in its lot with the formerly dominant nation. At first glance this appears to be the core of Lenin's program of national self-determination.[3]

36

Yet the apparent simplicity of the basic Leninist ideas on national self-determination is deceiving. In reality these ideas have many facets and pose many questions.

NATIONAL SELF-DETERMINATION—A DEMOCRATIC DEMAND

What prompted the Bolsheviks to adopt the slogan of the right of nations to self-determination? Recognition of the right to national self-determination is, Lenin asserts categorically, a democratic and a socialist demand and must be supported by the Party on both accounts.[4]

Why, according to Lenin, do "democratic and socialist tasks" obligate the proletariat and the Social-Democratic Party to support the principles of national self-determination? Let us first turn to the "democratic tasks" and then discuss the "socialist" ones.

In Lenin's writings on the nationality question such words as "democracy" and "democratic" figure prominently and recur often. Are we to conclude from the frequency of the references to "democracy" that the latter was precious to Lenin and had genuine ideological importance or should we dismiss it as having merely propagandistic or tactical significance?

Russian Marxists, including Lenin, had adopted Marx's and Engels' conception of the different stages of economic and social development. The bourgeois revolution, it was acknowledged, had not yet been completed in Russia. The socialist revolution therefore was even more distant. During the revolution of 1905 and thereafter Lenin accused the Russian bourgeoisie of selfishness and cowardice and maintained that it was neither able nor willing to complete the bourgeois-democratic revolution.[5] Therefore, the proletariat, a consistently revolutionary class, would itself have to make the bourgeois revolution. It had thus a dual task, a democratic and a socialist one, which were "indissolubly linked" with each other.[6]

National self-determination was a demand of bourgeois democracy. The consequent democrat must recognize the right of the oppressed nationalities to secession and to the formation of their own independent states. Not only socialists but all democrats were obligated to espouse the program of the right to national self-determination, meaning to secession. Liberty and democracy, Lenin asserted, were illusory, even for the dominant nationality, unless the reactionary and undemocratic Great Russian nationalism was curbed.[7]

Forcible retention of a nationality within the multinational state was, according to Lenin, undemocratic in all stages of social evolution. Since the national minorities of Russia prior to the peace of Brest Litovsk formed, as Lenin pointed out on several occasions, in the aggregate a majority of the population, denial of self-determination was thus an especially flagrant violation of democracy.

Of all political institutions under capitalism, Lenin held, democracy was the most developed and advanced form of government;[8] it was also the form of government most favorable for the proletariat and for the Social Democratic Party in the pursuance of their goals. It was in the interest of the proletariat to eliminate backward political forms for more advanced ones, such as political democracy, and to improve its strategic position for the final onrush against the capitalist fortress. Full democracy and capitalism were incongruous terms; yet the more democratic political institutions under capitalism would become, the stronger would be the base of the revolutionary proletariat. Lenin was then by no means indifferent to the type of political institutions under capitalism under which the proletariat and the Party were to operate.

These views emerge also clearly in Lenin's criticism of the position on the national question taken by Parabellum (Karl Radek) who had questioned the policy of national self-determination.

As to Comrade Parabellum, he, in the name of a socialist revolution, scornfully rejects a consistently revolutionary program in the realm of democracy. This is incorrect.

The proletariat cannot become victor save through democ-
racy, i.e. through introducing complete democracy and
through combining with every step of its movement demo-
cratic demands formulated most vigorously, most decisively.[9]

It would thus appear that Lenin considered bourgeois
political democracy a prerequisite of proletarian victory. Yet,
as the context reveals, Lenin merely maintained that the bourgeois-capitalist democracy would create "better conditions for
the class struggle"[10] of the proletariat. Socialism merely demanded a democratic program, democratic agitation and propaganda by the proletariat and the Party, "a consistently revolutionary formulation for each of our democratic demands."[11]

This is also made clear by the following. It is, Lenin insists,

quite conceivable that the workers of a certain country may
overthrow the bourgeoisie *before* even one fundamental
democratic reform has been accomplished in full. It is
entirely inconceivable, however, that the proletariat . . .
will be able to defeat the bourgeoisie if it is not prepared
for this task by being educated in the spirit of the most
consistent and determinedly revolutionary democracy.[12]

The latter demands also the propagation of the right of nations
to self-determination.

We must combine the revolutionary struggle against capitalism with a revolutionary program and revolutionary tactics
relative to *all* democratic demands: a republic, a militia,
officials elected by the people, equal rights for women, self-
determination of nations, etc. While capitalism exists, all
these demands are realizable only as an exception, and in an
incomplete, distorted form.[13]

The program of national self-determination is placed within
its larger context. The right to self-determination is a demand
of political democracy; it is one of many demands. The Party's
quest for self-determination is placed by Lenin on the same level

as the demand for a militia in contrast to a standing army, as the demand for equality of rights for women, etc. The proletariat, while advancing toward its goal of the proletarian revolution and of socialism, does not disdain to support the program of political democracy, backed ordinarily by the liberal bourgeoisie. It is admitted that under bourgeois capitalism all these ideas, including national self-determination, were realizable only as an "exception, and in an incomplete, distorted form." As a rule, the right to self-determination will not be attained prior to the "proletarian" revolution.

Only the "proletarian" revolution will create the foundation for the flowering of democracy, for the realization of "all democratic reforms."

> Basing ourselves on democracy, as it already exists, exposing its incompleteness under capitalism, we advocate the *overthrow of capitalism,* expropriation of the bourgeoisie, *as a necessary basis* both for the abolition of the poverty of the masses and *for a complete and manifold realization of all democratic reforms.* Some of these reforms will be started prior to the overthrow of the bourgeoisie, others in the process of the overthrow. . . . [14]

In the bourgeois-capitalist period self-determination will be "started" in some areas, but by no means everywhere. Lenin wanted the proletariat to raise the banner of self-determination in this stage. Most oppressed nationalities, however, were likely to make their decisions about their national future at the first opportune moment, that is, in the majority of cases, "in the process of the overthrow" of the capitalist regime, during the "proletarian" revolution. National self-determination under capitalism will be rather a rare phenomenon.[15]

Yet it does not follow that Social Democrats should therefore renounce the right to national self-determination in this stage. Abandoning the struggle for even one of the democratic reforms would be identical with playing into the hands of the bourgeoisie and of reaction.

It is apparent from the foregoing that Lenin was not swayed by merely propagandistic considerations—though the latter were always present—when he demanded national self-determination. He formulated this demand not only because it corresponded to the interests of the proletariat and of socialism, but also because it was required by democracy, by the needs of the bourgeois democratic revolution.

Political democracy under capitalism offers the proletariat, according to Lenin, the best opportunities for the class struggle against the bourgeoisie. Lenin calls political democracy "a freer, wider and more distinct form of class oppression," stressing its "significance," though, admittedly, it cannot "eliminate" capitalism. A consistent democratic propaganda and agitation, which included also the right to national self-determination, is, Lenin holds, a *sine qua non* first of a bourgeois democratic[16] and then of a "proletarian" victory. Both revolutions require making alliances between the proletariat and various dissatisfied and revolutionary democratic groups, including national minorities.[17] The program of self-determination, one of the demands of political democracy, is to cement the alliance of the proletariat with the mass of the oppressed nationalities.

The primary value of democracy is to Lenin clearly tactical, instrumental. It is little appreciated as such, but valued as a means to bring about the "proletarian" revolution and to attain the panacea of socialism. The propagation of political democracy, of each of the demands of democracy, including national self-determination, is looked upon as a necessity on tactical and ideological grounds, but basically on the former. Lenin's "ideology" itself is largely an elucidation of, a guide to, the right tactics.

While preferring political democracy,[18] Lenin by no means abandoned the idea of the dictatorship of the proletariat as a necessary stage prior to socialism. In the foregoing he had referred to political democracy of the bourgeois-capitalist era, revealing his preference for political democracy as opposed to other political forms. This preference appears to be based upon Lenin's conviction at the time that the proletarian army might advance more rapidly toward the goal of the "proletarian" revolution, dictatorship of the proletariat, and socialism, over the broad highway of bourgeois democracy rather than over the thorny paths of a politically backward, semi-feudal monarcho-authoritarian regime.

Yet political democracy, whatever its advantages for the proletariat, was then, Lenin held, non-existent in Russia. In Russia the "bourgeois-democratic revolution is not yet completed." Its completion is in the interest of the proletariat; it is "obligatory for Social Democrats," a "concrete task of the proletariat in the immediate future." [19] The bourgeoisie "will strive to disrupt and hinder" the impending revolution "and limit it to restricted democratic aims." The liberal bourgeoisie, Lenin explains in another connection, tends to become less democratic, since it fears the "proletarian" revolution; simultaneously, strong "nationalistic tendencies" [20] begin to envelop it.

The proletariat's "immediate task" is a bourgeois revolution, a "democratic revolution." [21] National self-determination, a democratic demand, must therefore be proclaimed immediately, not only for the sake of the proletarian and socialist revolution, but also for the sake of the more immediate "democratic revolution":

> The Russian proletariat cannot march at the head of the people towards the victorious democratic revolution (which is its immediate task) without demanding at once full and "rueckhaltlos" freedom of secession from Russia for all the nations oppressed by Tsarism. This we demand not as something separate from the revolutionary struggle for socialism, but because this struggle would remain an idle phrase if it were not linked up with a revolutionary approach to all the questions of democracy, including the national question.[22]

What Lenin again is primarily concerned with is a "revolutionary approach to all the questions of democracy, including the national question." Only such an approach will spell victory over the forces of autocracy in the impending democratic, political, bourgeois revolution.

As early as 1894 in his work *Who Are the Friends of the People?* Lenin had anticipated that the "Russian worker" "rising at the head of all the democratic elements" would "overthrow absolutism." [23] Some sort of alliance with "all democratic elements," though one led by the proletariat, was held to be a prerequisite to the success of the bourgeois democratic revolution. In 1897, in the article "The Tasks of Russian Social Democrats," Lenin had similarly written:

> In the democratic, the *political* struggle . . . the Russian working class does not stand alone. *Side by side* with the proletariat stand all the opposition elements of the bourgeoisie, or of the nationalities or religions and sects which are persecuted by the absolutist government.[24]

In the struggle in Russia prior to the bourgeois revolution and during the latter stage an alliance between the proletariat and, among others, the "persecuted" and oppressed nationalities, seemed imperative. This was Lenin's view in the last decade of the nineteenth century; it was also his view during the World War. The alliance was to be sealed by the program of national self-determination.

The opponents of the rights of nations to self-determination within the Party, the Left on the nationality question, criticized it primarily on two accounts. They maintained first that this program was bound to focus the attention of the oppressed nationalities on national issues instead of on the all-important issue of the "proletarian" seizure of power. They asserted secondly that self-determination, proclaimed under bourgeois capitalism, was not only harmful to proletarian interests, but also useless to the oppressed nationalities, since self-determination under conditions of imperialist capitalism was not realizable and was bound to remain an illusion.

Countering these criticisms of his and the Party's nationality program, Lenin stressed the importance of the Party's support for all "democratic demands." The proclamation of the right to secession would not distract the masses of the national minorities from the struggle for the "proletarian" seizure of power:

> It would be a fundamental mistake to suppose that the struggle for democracy can divert the proletariat from the socialist revolution, or obscure, or overshadow it, etc. To the contrary, just as socialism cannot be victorious unless it introduces complete democracy, so the proletariat will be unable to prepare for victory over the bourgeoisie unless it wages a many-sided, consistent and revolutionary struggle for democracy.[25]

A "many-sided" struggle "for democracy" requires that the proletariat does not lose sight of the national grievances of the oppressed national minorities:

> From the point of view of socialism, it is absolutely a mistake to ignore the tasks of national liberation in a situation of national oppression.[26]

Every weakness of the opponent, the ruling classes of the dominant nationalities, must be exploited, and no possible strengthening of the proletarian forces is to be neglected. Limiting proletarian interests to the distant "socialist revolution," instead of accelerating the historic tempo, might well delay it, while probing the enemy's long front, touching on all important issues, including the national one, might well result in detecting the weak spot in the enemy's armor and speed the coming of victory. Raising the national issue in the bourgeois-capitalist period is thus an imperative for the proletariat.[27]

Secondly, Lenin continues, it is argued by the "Marxist" opponents of the right to self-determination that it cannot be attained "within the framework of capitalism." [28] Lenin denies the truth of this statement. While admitting that the realization of self-determination would rather be an exception under capitalism, he holds it to be historically false to maintain that self-determination under capitalism cannot be realized at all; he points to Norway's separation from Sweden as evidence to the contrary. It would also be ridiculous to deny that with only

> a little change of the political and strategic relations, e.g. of Germany and Great Britain, the formation of new states, perhaps of a Polish, an Indian state or other states, would become a possibility today or to-morrow.[29]

While the elimination of steadily recurring economic crises under capitalism is held to be an illusion, it is believed incorrect to say that self-determination of nationalities was "just as" [30] impossible of realization.

Lenin admits that only a few oppressed nationalities are likely to attain national independence in this period. One among fifty, or even one among a hundred nationalities, might perhaps liberate itself before the socialist revolution, he holds on one occasion.[31] The right of the oppressed nationality to secession, however, must be acknowledged by the proletariat of the oppressor nationality, he writes another time,

> even when this separation before the victory of the revolution were only possible . . . in one case among thousands.[32]

In general, he holds, the liberation of the colonies can only be "realized simultaneously with socialism." [33]

Yet whatever the likelihood of the fulfillment of national liberation under capitalism, Lenin emphasizes that nothing could possibly be more damaging to the Social Democratic Party than abandoning "one of the points of the democratic program," namely self-determination of nations, merely on account of its "supposedly 'illusory' character in the imperialist epoch." [34] National self-determination is tactically a most valuable weapon, and the Party must be aware of the importance of a truly revolutionary slogan.

Considering the assumption that national self-determination would remain under capitalism rather "an exception," Lenin has devoted a very large amount of his writing on the nationality question to the bourgeois-capitalist stage.[35] It could be argued that he considered education of the proletariat in internationalism so vital for the later stages of the proletarian revolution, of proletarian dictatorship, of socialism and communism, that he wished to begin it under capitalism. Education of the proletariat in internationalism in the bourgeois-capitalist stage is indeed duly stressed by Lenin. Yet, as he makes amply clear, "education" of the proletariat begins—and ends—with the analysis and elucidation of the slogan of the right to national self-determination. "Education" and propaganda are hardly distinguished. Long-range educational and short-range tactical objectives are well served by the same means, the propagation of the slogan of national self-determination.

Lenin never fails to point out the immediate tactical usefulness of the slogan. While the ultimate goal is never lost sight of, the significance of the slogan of national self-determination does lie less in its future "educational" value and more in its immediate impact upon the proletariat's fighting capacity. The latter is of sufficient importance to Lenin to justify his giving the most detailed attention to the Party's nationality policy in the bourgeois-capitalist stage.

Under capitalism the program of the right to national self-determination, meaning to secession—the chances of realization of which, in spite of repeated references to the example of Norway, were held definitely slim in this stage—seemed then to have had tactical and propaganda value rather than genuine ideological significance. Which function, according to Lenin's thought, it was to serve in the later stages, the "proletarian" revolution, the "proletarian" dictatorship, and socialism, remains to be seen.

National Self-Determination—
A Proletarian-Socialist Imperative

The right to self-determination is held by Lenin to be not only a "democratic" but also a "socialist" imperative. "Socialist tasks" too demand of the proletariat the program of national self-determination.

Why does Lenin consider the right to national self-determination a "socialist" demand? Basically, because socialism and continued national oppression are held to be irreconcilable.[36] Socialism aims at the elimination of oppression on economic and social grounds. It cannot accept national oppression—whether brought about centuries ago or in the more recent era of renewed imperialist expansion—and rejects domination of one nation by the other.[37] The specific arguments presented by Lenin may be grouped under the following four headings:

(1) To proclaim the right of all nations to secession means to recognize the equality of all nations. Such a proclamation will establish national harmony and unity within the Party and among the proletariat[38] of a multinational state such as Russia, will turn the Party into an offensive fighting instrument of the working class and thus speed the coming of the "proletarian," of the socialist revolution.

(2) The program of national self-determination will not only strengthen the Party, but also will secure for the working class other than proletarian allies from among the oppressed nationalities and thus accelerate the advent of the "proletarian" revolution.

(3) The Party's national program is the best means of "fighting nationalism"[39] and of "educating"[40] the fighting proletariat in internationalism. Such education is necessary if the proletariat is to seize power and to establish socialism on a world scale.

(4) After the "proletarian" revolution, the Party's policy of national self-determination will eliminate national strife among

the nationalities of the multinational state[41] as well as among nations themselves and thus help to strengthen the proletarian dictatorship and later socialism.

The argument may be summed up thus: The policy of national self-determination is bound to strengthen the Party, gain allies for the "proletariat," further internationalism during the bourgeois-capitalist period, and also accomplish some of these very purposes during the later stages of proletarian dictatorship and socialism. This policy is a "socialist task" and imperative, because it is in the interests of socialism, will speed its oncoming, and, once the new order has been established, will strengthen its foundation.

Points 2 and 4 will be elaborated later.[42] Points 1 and 3 will be discussed in the following:

Point (1): The Party's program of nationality must be centered around the right to self-determination, meaning to secession, around the right of all nations to their national state.[43] The program will strengthen class "solidarity"[44] among the workers of the diverse nationalities in the state and solidify "the alliance of all proletarians of all nations." The Party, of course, plays a key role in the "proletarian" revolution. It is the vanguard of the working class prior to, during, and after the "proletarian" revolution. It is the weapon without which the proletariat cannot attain victory and cannot reach socialism. For Lenin, to work continuously toward, to forge the "unity"[45] of the proletariat and of the Party is therefore always the most urgent task. For this reason, in a multinational state such as Russia the Party must stand unequivocally for national equality and reject any kind of national discrimination.

This is the more important since the Russian ruling classes attempt to confuse and divide the proletariat. They try to "divert" the attention of the masses from their pressing social problems and "real enemies" to the alleged foreign foe and to mislead the proletariat with nationalist slogans by "stirring up

hatred"[46] against other nationalities. The "Black-Hundred Nationalism"[47] endeavors to pit nationality against nationality to stave off the impending revolution. The task of the Social Democratic Party and of the proletariat must therefore consist in carrying on a relentless struggle against all divisive nationalist manoeuvres by proclaiming national equality.

The right to national self-determination is a true criterion of national equality. It assures all nationalities freedom of separation, freedom of choice concerning their national future, and eliminates force and compulsion from the relations between the nationalities of the polyglot states. This assurance, Lenin holds, will have an immediately beneficial, a conciliatory, effect upon all nationalities concerned.

Point (3): Education of the proletariat in internationalism and struggle against national prejudices of every sort are imperatives for the proletariat of the oppressor as well as for that of the oppressed nationalities. Internationalism is more than an ultimate goal; it is an immediate necessity, an urgent task. Both members of the oppressor and oppressed nationalities are prejudiced, yet the prejudice of the former appears to Lenin the more serious one. It is the one which must be overcome if national self-determination is to become a reality. Individuals belonging to the oppressor nations were "throughout school and life" brought up "in a spirit of contempt or deprecation of the workers of the oppressed nations." And Lenin continues in a somewhat autobiographical vein:

> Every Great Russian who has been educated among Great Russians or has lived among them has experienced this.[48]

The Social Democratic Party is duty-bound to

> educate the workers to be 'indifferent' to national distinctions. Nobody will dispute that. But not to be indifferent in the spirit of the annexationists. A member of an oppressing nation must be 'indifferent' to whether small nations belong to *his* state or to a *neighboring* state or to themselves,

according to where their sympathies lie. If he is not 'indifferent' in this way, he is *not* a Social Democrat; one must *not* think only of one's own nation, but must place the interests of all nations, their general liberty and equality, *above one's own nation.*[49]

It is precisely the propaganda of the right of nations to self-determination which guarantees the democratic and socialist education of the masses.

Only such propaganda ensures the maximum chances of national peace in Russia should it remain a heterogenous nation state; and such propaganda ensures the most peaceful (and for the proletarian struggle, harmless) division into the various national states, should the question of such division arise.[50]

National antipathies will not vanish in the foreseeable future, but only after the victory of socialism. The struggle to overcome national suspicion and hate, however, must be commenced immediately, Lenin concluded:

If we want to remain loyal to socialism, we must *now* take care of the *international education of the masses* which, as far as oppressed nationalities are concerned, is impossible without the propagation of the freedom of separation of the oppressed nationalities.[51]

The "freedom of separation," the right to self-determination, emerges thus as a cure-all; it is essential as an instrument of propaganda of the proletariat in the capitalist era, as a right of the oppressed nationality and a possible goal before and, if insisted upon, after the "proletarian" revolution, and as an effective means of educating[52] the proletariat in a truly international spirit.

Recognition of the right of nations to self-determination, while in general to be justified on the basis of political democracy and of proletarian and socialist interests, constitutes also a recognition of the vitality of nationalism. It is in several ways an encouragement of nationalism, though an encouragement of the cause of national liberty, and not of an imperialist and exploiting nationalism. Against the criticism of the Left that the slogan of the right to national self-determination appeared to " 'offer' the maximum to nationalism," Lenin counters by saying that "in reality the recognition of the *right* of *all* nations to self-determination is the maximum of *democracy* and the minimum of nationalism." [53] Furthermore, nationalism is held under some circumstances, and for some time, to be an ally of the proletariat. Lenin could also have assured the Left that the terms of the alliance were to be written by himself and the Bolshevik Party.

While the national liberation movement in general is rather favorably looked upon as a potential ally of the proletariat of the dominant, imperialist, economically advanced nationality, Lenin intended not to permit even a progressive and liberal national movement to weaken proletarian class-consciousness and not to allow a socialist-inspired plan for the reorganization of the Party along national lines, as propagated by Austrian and Russian socialists including the Bund, to undermine the Party, the fighting instrument of the proletariat.

Against Bourgeois and "Socialist" Nationalism

National culture is the program put forward by the liberal bourgeoisie of the oppressed nationalities to further their growth and development. It has obvious cultural and national objectives and often also clearly political goals, namely the formation of a separate political entity. Since its appeal is to all members of the nationality, it tends to bridge class differences. It purports to reduce the class struggle by linking the proletariat with all other classes in common endeavors.

National culture in the capitalist stage, however, was, according to Lenin, a bourgeois culture and had therefore to be rejected by the proletariat. The Party was bent on widening the gulf between the working masses and the bourgeoisie in preparation for the final struggle for the seizure of power.

What, according to Lenin, is the role of the liberal bourgeoisie in the national movement? Depending on the stage of social and national development, the bourgeoisie plays first a progressive part, in accordance with its program of political democracy, but later an increasingly reactionary one; it shelves democracy out of fear that the bourgeois democratic revolution would quickly usher in the socialist revolution. In the first phase, the proletariat, though never abandoning its own interests and always pursuing its own goals, is willing to give the liberal bourgeoisie some support. In the later phase, however, when the "bourgeoisie stretches its hands out to the landlords and to the police" and its "inconsistency and opportunism" reveal themselves, the proletariat is obligated to refuse any assistance. It then becomes "evident to everybody" that the bourgeoisie acts

> in the question of the universal state language as also in a whole series of other similar questions treasonably, hypocritically, and idiotically (even from the point of view of the interests of liberalism).[54]

The conclusion may therefore be drawn that at this stage

> *every* liberal-bourgeois nationalism carries into the proletarian ranks the greatest demoralization and causes the greatest injury to the cause of liberty and of the proletarian class struggle . . . It is in *the name and the slogan* of 'national culture'—of Great Russian, Polish, Jewish, Ukrainian culture—that the Black-Hundreds, the Clericals, and then also the bourgeois of *all nationalities* carry on their reactionary, dirty business.[55]

The slogan of "national culture" and similar ones have a definite class content and have to be judged on this basis, and not on the basis of "general principles." National culture, unmistakably, is a weapon of the bourgeoisie.[56]

Reference is made by Lenin to a Bundist of the name of Libmann who held that the worker ought not to be indifferent to the development of his nationality's culture, since it is only by means of his national culture that he is enabled to participate in the international culture of democracy and of the proletarian movement of all countries. Libmann's assertion that international culture is not anational, not a culture without specific national form, is acknowledged by Lenin. Then, however, he parts ways with Libmann. There were in every national culture, he asserts,

> *elements* of democratic and socialist culture, since every nationality had a proletarian and exploited mass of people whose conditions of life unavoidably produce a democratic and socialist ideology. But in *every* nationality there exists also a bourgeois culture (and in the majority of cases still an arch-reactionary and clerical one) and not only in the form of 'elements,' but also as a *prevailing* culture. Therefore 'national culture' in general *is* the culture of the agrarians, of the clerics, and of the bourgeoisie . . . If we proclaim the slogan of the 'international culture of democracy and the proletarian movement of the entire world,' we take from *every* national culture *only* its democratic and socialist elements; we take only these and *only exclusively* as counterweight against the bourgeois culture, against the bourgeois nationalism of *every* nationality.[57]

National culture is, as stated, a bourgeois slogan, a weapon of the bourgeoisie. It is in the interest of militant bourgeois nationalism to deceive the workers and disunite them with its help. He, however, who wishes to serve the proletariat and the cause of socialism, must unite the workers of the different nationalities and consistently fight bourgeois nationalism, his "own" nationalism as well as the alien one. He who defends the slogan of national culture belongs to the nationalist petty bourgeoisie, not to the Marxists. "It is by no means our task to proclaim and tolerate the slogan of 'national culture'." [58]

Lenin stresses what he calls the "democratic and socialist elements" in each national culture. The aggregate of the "elements," the proletarian, democratic, and socialist elements of the individual national cultures, constitutes the "international culture of democracy and of the proletarian movement."

There exists, of course, no international culture "of democracy and of the proletarian movement," unless it is expressed in the language of a specific nationality. There is no international culture of the proletariat, expressed, for instance, in Esperanto. If Lenin's juxtaposition of the bourgeois "elements" of each individual nationality with "international culture" is to have any concrete meaning at all, it is the juxtaposition of the bourgeois "elements" of each individual nationality with its proletarian-democratic cultural elements, of bourgeois and proletarian ideas, of capitalist and socialist ideology in a broader sense of the word. The proletarian and socialist ideology is "only the counterweight against the bourgeois culture." There is a struggle taking place within each national culture, within the political framework of each nation, and it is carried on in the language of the respective people.

The juxtaposition of national with international culture in Lenin's writings had very likely propagandistic significance. It may have served the purpose of arousing class-consciousness in the proletariat and of setting the working class of the oppressed nationality apart from its bourgeoisie and other classes. As such it had meaning and purpose. Yet international culture, as Lenin admitted, was not without national color and character; it could be expressed only through the media of national cultures. The furtherance of international culture did by no means require retrogression of national cultures nor their standstill. To the contrary, the flourishing of national culture could go hand in hand with the spread of international culture. Lenin admitted once that national culture might be interpreted in some way not contrary to internationalism.[59] It rather appears therefore that Lenin, in the interest and for the sake of propagandistic brevity and of political appeal, preferred a juxtaposition of national with international culture which, logically, was not warranted.

In the entire bourgeois-capitalist period the proletariat and the Party were, according to Lenin, not only opposed to national culture, a weapon of the bourgeoisie, but also to extra-territorial national-cultural autonomy. The latter was a concrete project for the solution of the national problem, advanced in the early twentieth century by the Austian socialists; this "Austrian heresy" [60] had found many adherents among Social Democrats in Russia, especially the Jewish Bund, Caucasian socialists, and others.

Both programs, national culture and extra-territorial national-cultural autonomy, simply called by Lenin national-cultural autonomy, threatened to weaken the class-consciousness of the proletariat and to undermine its will to fight.[61] National-cultural autonomy in particular threatened to destroy the unitary, centralized Party structure and thus to dull the edges of the sharpest weapon which the proletariat possessed.

After the turn of the century, the Austrian Social Democratic writers Karl Renner and Otto Bauer had, as previously mentioned, suggested a program which would satisfy the various Austrian nationalities, reconcile them with the multinational state, and thus maintain the integrity of the large Austrian economic realm. Nationality, according to them, was no longer tied up with territory. Members of a national group which lived scattered throughout Austria's realm—a consequence of considerable internal migration—were, they held, as much entitled to national rights as those concentrated in one or several regions. The Austrian theoreticians did not wish to deny national rights, the rights to their own schools and to preserving their language and culture, to ethnic groups which, though dispersed throughout the empire, had retained strong national ties and wanted to preserve and develop their nationality. Their program of extra-territorial national-cultural autonomy consisted in granting the benefits of national rights to all interested individuals of a nationality, wherever their habitat.[62]

The concept of extra-territorial national-cultural autonomy appeared to Lenin disruptive of the tight centralistic Party organization, largely because it rested not on a strictly territorial basis, but on an individual-national one; this circumstance, no doubt, would have complicated the transmission and execution of directives from central headquarters. The Bund's claim at the Second Congress of the Party in 1903 to be recognized as sole representative of the Jewish proletariat "in whatever part of Russia" it lived and "whatever language" [63] it spoke, would, if accepted, have split the Party along national lines and, in Lenin's view, would have weakened and destroyed it.

National-cultural autonomy appeared to Lenin irreconcilable with the conception of a strictly centralistic, unitary Party organization, with "democratic centralism," the vaunted Bolshevik principle. The latter, however, seemed to permit the existence of regional, territorial Party units which were either ethnically homogenous or in which one or the other national minority prevailed. These regional groupings were the arms of the central headquarters and were to carry out the center's orders.

National-cultural autonomy not only ran counter to "democratic centralism." It also *"strengthened,"* as Karl Kautsky had aptly pointed out, "nationalism and *neglected* internationalism completely." [64] This, according to Lenin, became especially apparent in the suggestion of a separate education for the different nationalities.

The essence of the plan of "so-called national-cultural autonomy" consisted in "separation of schooling according to nationalities."

> Every nationality, irrespective of the place of residence of a member, forms a single union, which is recognized by the state, a union in charge of national-cultural affairs.

The "most important of these matters is schooling." According to the plan, "every citizen" registers "voluntarily" with some national union.

Such a separation of schooling, Lenin asserts,

> is impermissible from the viewpoint of democracy in general and from the interests of the proletarian class struggle in particular . . . As long as different nationalities live in one state, they are linked with each other by millions and billions of ties of an economic and legal character as well as by the entire way of life. How can one separate schooling from this context 'and withdraw it from the competence of the state'? To the contrary, one must strive in education for the amalgamation of nations so that that be prepared in school which is realized in life.[65]

"From the viewpoint of the proletarian class struggle," the separation of education along national lines must be opposed by Social Democracy.

In almost every capitalist enterprise, Lenin adds revealingly,

> mines and plants, trade firms and capitalist agricultural enterprises, workers presented a most varied national picture.[66]

The factory is thus placed alongside the school. Clearly, if schooling is to be separated along national lines, the organization of workers in factories in nationally mixed regions might follow this precedent. No wonder that Lenin sharply opposes the concept of national-cultural autonomy which threatened in more than one way to undermine the unitary and centralistic Party structure.

The main arguments thus presented against national-cultural autonomy were that this project strengthened nationalism against internationalism and united proletariat and bourgeoisie, instead of keeping them apart; it worked thus at cross purposes with the proletariat fighting for socialism.

Considerations bearing on the class struggle were of some importance in Lenin's bitter denunciations of national culture. Similar considerations bearing also on the organization of the Party were paramount in his criticism of national-cultural autonomy. The latter

> *unifies* the proletariat and the bourgeoisie of *one* nation and *separates* the proletarians of the *different* nationalities.[67]

The importance of organization as an element in Lenin's and the Bolshevik Party's rejection of national-cultural autonomy is clearly brought out in the following remark by Stalin in 1913:

> The type of organization . . . is a tremendous agitational factor on behalf of internationalism . . . When the workers are organized according to nationality they are isolated within their national shells, fenced off from each other by the organizational partitions. The stress is laid not on what is *common* to the workers, but on what distinguishes them from each other.[68]

As early as 1894 in *Who Are the Friends of the People?* Lenin had emphasized the vital importance of the "amalgamation" of national proletarian organizations:

> There is no other way of combatting national hatred than by organizing and uniting the oppressed class for the struggle against the oppressor class in each separate country and by the amalgamation of such national working-class organizations into a single working-class army to fight international capitalism.

In 1903 in the article "Does the Jewish Proletariat Need an Independent Political Party?" Lenin endorsed a tightly organized centralistic Party and rejected a party organization which was based on federal-national lines:

> We must rely upon the entire proletariat without difference as to language and nationality. We must not create any

organizations which march separately, which go their own
ways. No alienation, no isolation must be carried into our
ranks.[69]

Centralism was "necessary" for a "successful struggle against the
autocracy." [70] The special oppression suffered by the Jewish
workers, which was admitted by Lenin,[71] merely emphasized, he
pointed out later, the "necessity of the most close union between
the workers of the different nationalities." [72] A strongly centralized Party was always held by Lenin to be a *sine qua non* of
"proletarian" victory.

Lenin rejected the concept of national-cultural autonomy
for the organization of the *Party,* since he feared its corrosive
effects upon the "proletarian" fighting machine; he was convinced of the ineffectiveness of an organization which was based
upon federal and national lines. He also rejected the concept of
national-cultural autonomy for the proletarian *state,* likewise on
the ground of its incompatibility with the principle of centralism,
in his opinion the only feasible form of government for the
"proletarian" dictatorship. In addition, the project of national-
cultural autonomy seemed to him who favored physical and cultural assimilation—which he believed to be in the interests of
the proletariat and of socialism—to delay unduly this natural
process and to encourage nationalism.

NATIONAL SELF-DETERMINATION—AND ASSIMILATION

Nationalism will be combatted not merely by the nationality policy of the Social Democratic Party, namely national self-
determination, but also by a natural process, the assimilation of
ethnic groups. This process is operative in the capitalist era and
will continue to be in operation after the "proletarian" revolution and also during the stage of socialism.

Lenin hails this natural process[73] in all stages. It is as if he
were pleased that nature—assimilation, amalgamation of ethnic
groups—has come to his, rather the proletariat's, assistance to

diminish national differences and facilitate the growth of international harmony by simply reducing the number of nationalities.

A conception of the scope of the assimilation of nationalities under modern capitalism may be gained, Lenin holds, by glancing at the immigration statistics of the United States. The state of New York, not merely the metropolis, was said to be a melting pot:

> And what happens in large, international scope in New York, occurs in *every* big city and in every factory.

He who "is not steeped in national prejudices," will have to acknowledge that this

> process of assimilation of nationalities through capitalism constitutes a tremendous historic progress, the destruction of national ossification in the various distant regions, especially in the backward regions of Russia.[74]

In the essay "Critical Notes on the National Question" Lenin noticed a "world-historic tendency of capitalism" which pointed to the "tearing down of national differences, to the assimilation of nationalities." This tendency "emerged increasingly powerful" and represented "one of the greatest driving forces to turn capitalism into socialism." [75] In his enthusiasm for assimilation, Lenin tended to exaggerate its role in the emergence of the "proletarian" revolution. It is difficult to perceive why the mere reduction in the number of nationalities should speed the coming of the "proletarian" revolution and of socialism.

By no means did Lenin hold it to be the task of the Party to assist the cultural growth of nationalities in any stage of social development:

> The proletariat not only does not undertake to fight for the national development of every nation, but . . . warns the masses against such illusions.[76]

Since the historical trend disclosed the assimilation of nationalities to each other and the submergence of many of them, the development and fostering of their national culture would be rather a step backward. Neither during the proletarian struggle under capitalism nor, as shall be shown, after the seizure of power or in the stage of socialism, is multiplicity of nationalities and national cultures desirable. The opposite is the case. Yet force as a means of bringing about assimilation is decisively rejected, no doubt for the reason that it would defeat its purpose.

Lenin's position in regard to nationalism, national culture, and assimilation also emerged clearly in his criticism of the views of an Ukrainian Social Democrat named Lev Yurkevich. Lenin professed to discern in the latter's nationality policy the unmistakable criterion of petty-bourgeois nationalism. Yurkevich, according to Lenin, had admitted that only a minority among Ukrainian workers was "national-minded," while the majority was under the influence of Great Russian culture. Yurkevich held it to be part of the national program of the Ukrainian Social Democrats to instill Ukrainian culture[77] into the masses and to "make clear to them" their " 'national tasks'." On this account Lenin took him to task. A conscious national effort would counteract the natural process of assimilation and run counter to proletarian interests. Yurkevich, Lenin scolded, acted like

a narrow-minded and stupid bourgeois . . . if he rejects the interests of union, of amalgamation and assimilation of the proletariat of two nations for a passing success of the Ukrainian national cause.[78]

Lenin expected the Ukrainians sooner or later to throw in their lot with Russia. He repeatedly excoriated opposition to assimilation. He held assimilation to be "decidedly" "a progressive fact." [79]

This general view colored also Lenin's opinions about the Jews. Unlike many other nationalities, they lived scattered throughout Russia, and not in compact settlement along the frontiers.

Lenin apparently had made up his mind that the Jews would be better off by assimilating themselves. He criticized the Bundists' demand for the creation of institutions which would "guarantee" the freedom of Jewish national development.[80] He did not wish to be a party to "guarantee" the continued existence and development of any nationality. Lenin hoped that many nationalities would follow the road leading to assimilation, though he did not recommend it outright as a solution of the nationality problem. In his opinion, the Jews in civilized countries were no nationality any longer. In Galicia and Russia they were not yet a nationality; they were there, "unfortunately, still a caste." [81] Under these circumstances his demand for their assimilation was not illogical.

"Union, amalgamation, and assimilation" are held out to be desirable goals, though sometimes these words are used with special reference to the proletariat only of the various nationalities.

> The workers of the oppressed nationalities . . . must consider the demand for unity and amalgamation of the workers of the oppressed nationalities with the workers of the oppressor nations as their main task.[82]

In another connection Lenin assigns to the proletariat the task to support

> unconditional unity and complete amalgamation of the workers of *all* unions, cooperatives, consumer and cultural associations and other workers' organizations.[83]

The stress is here on "amalgamation" of the proletariat of the diverse nationalities in joint proletarian organizations.[84] What is to be brought about is greater organizational unity of the working class. The significance, however, of merely formal organizational unity is not to be assessed lightly. The organizational unity of the proletariat of the diverse nationalities would,

Lenin thought, have a powerful assimilatory impact upon all nationalities, would weaken the national consciousness of the individual workers and, in general, loosen their national ties. Assimilation, Lenin held, would be a by-product of the merger of national workers' organizations, of the establishment of a united workers' Party. Amalgamation of the different national workers' organizations under capitalism would bring about a de-emphasis of natural differences in national character and in outlook, and spur assimilation of nationalities.

Lenin's policy of nationality in the stages prior to the "proletarian" revolution recognizes a kind of status quo as to the level of national culture and the number of nationalities. Lenin does not pursue a course which leads to arresting the growth of national culture or to the curtailing of existing nationalities, though he favors assimilation. He is neither inclined to resort to force to reduce the number of nationalities for the purpose of compulsory assimilation—the policy of many a chauvinism—nor to further their increase for the sake of ethnic-cultural pluralism. He rather looks favorably upon assimilation of nationalities as the unavoidable historical trend, the inevitable result of the spread of the idea of national equality and of increasing economic and cultural interchange.

From the viewpoint of cultural and national pluralism, the disappearance of any nationality, like that of any biological species, is regrettable. The adherent of ethnic pluralism welcomes ethnic variety and cultural diversity and laments the death of any nationality, whether it is brought about by physical destruction and violence or in the natural process of assimilation. Lenin, however, does not share this opinion. His view is not that of the esthetician, partial to ethnic multiplicity, but that of the tactician of the "proletarian" revolution. Though he does not directly hold that the existence of more nationalities means greater obstacles on the road to the proletariat's seizure of power, his theoretical opposition to nationalism and his political sensitivity make him wary of the increase of nationalism and of the number of nationalities. A larger number of nationalities means at least the *possibility* of more, and more intense, national movements.

Lenin claims impartiality in regard to ethnic pluralism, but he is clearly opposed to it, placing his hopes on the natural, unavoidable process of assimilation, even expecting from it a speeding toward socialism. Assimilation is held "one of the greatest driving forces to turn capitalism into socialism," [85] a statement hardly reconcilable with the Marxist viewpoint. Lenin's actual opposition to ethnic pluralism may be an expression of his fear lest nationalism become a rival to the socialist movement[86] rather than a support to the proletarian Party in its struggle for socialism. Also, in his rejection of national pluralism and his undissimulated joy over assimilation of nationalities, Lenin may have been motivated by the fear that national strife was not merely the result of economic dissensions and of the class struggle[87]—bound to disappear with the latter—but partly at least, the result of innate national differences.

The Party's slogan of national self-determination constitutes, as previously stated, a recognition of the importance of nationality and nationalism. Lenin's wholehearted approval of the struggle against national subjection—"To a struggle against any national oppression we say absolutely 'yes' " [88]—signifies, however, not only rejection of the oppression of nationalities, but recognition of their equality, recognition, at least as a matter of fact, of nationalism and of the national state. The Party's slogan of national self-determination stimulates, to a degree, national impulses and national drives. It represents a concession to nationalism.

Lenin's encouragement of nationalism contradicts his real conviction that retrogression of nationalism, assimilation of nationalities, the disappearance of one or the other ethnic group, are beneficial to the proletariat. Fostering of national culture is decisively rejected: "To a struggle *for* any national development, *for* a 'national culture' in general, we say absolutely 'no'." [89] His stress on international rather than national culture—whether under bourgeois capitalism or, as will have to be shown, under the proletarian state—his joy over assimilation and his support of amalgamation of nationalities at any stage of their development—all this establishes a clear pattern, a pattern of negativism, of rejection of nationalism, of nationality, and of national culture; a pattern which is difficult to reconcile with his insistence on national self-determination, his "approval" of the national state.

Lenin's concession to nationalism, tactically motivated, was to have only transient significance; it was, he held, bound to redound in the end to the advantage of internationalism. Even if the Bolshevik slogan of national self-determination should lead to the creation of one or the other independent state under capitalism, or, as remains to be shown, during or after the "proletarian" revolution, the nationality concerned might later rejoin the fold of the multinational state. Prior to it, the slogan was expected to rally the dependent and oppressed nationalities to the side of the proletariat of the oppressor nationality, to the side also of the Great Russian proletariat.

NATIONAL SELF-DETERMINATION—AND THE ADVANTAGES OF THE LARGE STATE

While Lenin espoused the principle of national self-determination, he favored assimilation of nationalities; while he upheld the right to separation, he also extolled the advantages of the large economic capitalist state for the proletariat. The large state was often the multinational bourgeois-capitalist or semi-feudal state; the state, the borders of which were likely to recede in case of the secession of a border nationality.

Marx and Engels had been opponents of petty states. In the nineteenth century they had favored the national unification movements of the German and other nationalities. They had held that larger economic and political units were better political arenas for the unavoidable class struggle between proletariat and bourgeoisie.

Lenin shared Marx's and Engels' objections to the small state and their predilection for the larger state. "Under otherwise equal conditions," Lenin wrote in the "Critical Notes on the National Question," the class-conscious proletariat would "always support a bigger state." It would

> hail the close economic unity of large realms in which the battle of the proletariat against the bourgeoisie may develop on a broad basis.[90]

The rapid development of the productive forces of capitalism demanded large states in which the

> bourgeoisie will tear down all old, medieval . . . local, and narrowly national barriers of status, religious belief, and of other kinds.

Because capitalism, unknowingly, in these respects smoothed the road to socialism, the proletariat would heartily approve and further this development in the bourgeois-capitalist era.

In the capitalist stage Lenin favors not only a large state over a small one, but also centralization over federalism and decentralization:

> The large centralized state is a tremendous historic step ahead on the way from medieval disintegration to the future socialist unity of the entire world, and another way to socialism than over such a state (with capitalism indissolubly linked) does not exist and cannot exist.[91]

The large centralized state under capitalism does not only provide the best conditions for a proletarian revolution, but, as Lenin here at least suggests, the only one.

On the one hand Lenin maintained that the large capitalist state was preferable for the fighting proletariat; on the other hand he presented the right to self-determination in the bourgeois stage as an imperative for the workers. How could, according to Lenin, the proletariat in the bourgeois stage support the slogan of the right to national self-determination, to secession, if the large state was the "only road to socialism"? Even if Lenin has here overstated his case, how could the proletariat uphold national self-determination if, in any case, the large state was preferable to the small one? Was secession under capitalism so unlikely? Did Lenin and the Party espouse the slogan in the hope that its adoption would not lead to the disintegration of the multinational state, either during the bourgeois-capitalist stage or thereafter?

Lenin held indeed that only few oppressed nationalities would actually attain national independence in the bourgeois-capitalist period and would set up new states. On one occasion, as already stated, he voiced the opinion that only one among fifty or even one hundred nationalities would secure independence before the "proletarian" revolution.[92] If, therefore, the tactical advantages and some of the disadvantages of the slogan of the right of nationalities to self-determination in the capitalist period were to be balanced, there was little doubt for Lenin where the advantages lay. Besides, he seems to have believed that the disadvantage, the destruction or diminishing of the large state, was only a temporary one. Lenin appears to have been convinced that secession, if it should occur in one or the other case under capitalism or after the "proletarian" seizure of power, would prove to be merely a fleeting phenomenon, only a temporary setback, and political "amalgamation" would always be the ultimate end.

This, in fact, becomes evident in his comment on Marx's position in regard to Ireland and the national question:

> Marx never was in favor of small states, or of splitting up states, or of the federation principles. Still he considered the separation of an oppressed nation as a step of nations towards concentration, but concentration on the basis of democracy.[93]

Marx, according to Lenin, looked here upon the separation of the Irish people as "a step towards federation," "towards concentration," though one on a voluntary basis. One would have expected that "separation" rather meant what the word seemed to convey, that it signified diminution of the state's territories. Yet Marx, according to Lenin, and one might add, Lenin himself, did not stress the more immediate and obvious results of separation—which must have been of doubtful value to both. Its immediate results—new small states—were no doubt in accordance with national self-determination and with political democracy, but had to be regretted from the viewpoint of internationalism, of economy, and of broader proletarian interests, all of which required a large state. Lenin's view, however, was a long-range one. At the moment of the apparent victory of negative centrifugal trends he already saw the promising beginning of beneficial centripetal tendencies which would not only restore the previous large multinational state, but even lead beyond it.

> To defend this right [to secession] does in no way mean encouraging the formation of small states, but, to the contrary, it leads to a freer, . . . wider formation of larger states—a phenomenon more advantageous for the masses and more in accord with economic development.[94]

The right to secession is no encouragement of secession; "to the contrary," granting this right will rather strengthen the ties of the nationalities with the multinational state and perhaps will attract neighboring nationalities and bring about a "wider formation" of "larger states."

In another connection Lenin maintained that the free separation of Norway from Sweden "has created the basis for a much closer, much more democratic state." The secession produced a new state, yet Lenin saw already laid the basis for a "more democratic state,"—*one* state, it should be noted.

Similarly, Lenin, in May, 1917, stressing the "right of all nationalities which are now part of the Russian state freely to separate and to form independent states," held that the "Republic of the Russian people should draw to itself other peoples or nationalities, not through violence, but through voluntary mutual agreement to build a *common* state." [95]

Lenin was convinced of the advantages for the proletariat of the large economic realm not only under bourgeois capitalism but also, as will be shown later, under the proletarian dictatorship and socialism. If he, nevertheless, clung to the concept of the right to national self-determination, he did so because he was persuaded that the benefits of such a policy by the Party would far exceed any harm it was likely to cause. Secession under capitalism, he held, was after all not very likely, but if it should become a reality, it would turn out to be a short-lived one; it would prove merely a stepping stone "towards federation," "towards concentration," and would lead to an even "wider formation" of "larger states." The program of national self-determination would thus be tactically vindicated.

TACTICAL PROBLEMS. THE PRIMACY OF SOCIALISM

In the bourgeois-capitalist stage the proletariat, according to Lenin, is not to neglect any vital political, economic, or social issue which could be successfully exploited and be made to strengthen the proletarian base and proletarian forces under capitalism. It is also not to neglect the problem of national oppression.[96] At the same time it was understood that any possible rivalry between nationalism and socialism was to be concluded in favor of the latter and at the expense of the former.

In discussing Marx's position on the relation of socialism and nationalism, Lenin's own views emerge clearly:

> Compared to the labor question the subordinate significance of the question of nationality for Marx was beyond doubt. Yet this theory is removed sky-high from ignoring national movements.[97]

Marx had criticized "the Proudhon-clique" which had declared nationalities as "non-sense," though he thought its activities and polemics against chauvinism "useful and understandable." [98]

Lenin approves wholeheartedly what he considers Marx's middle-of-the-road policy in the nationality question. The characteristics of this policy lie in subordinating the question of nationality to the general interests of socialism and of the proletariat of all nationalities, while not "ignoring" vital national movements. Lenin, believing he followed the example of Marx, takes to task both the Left and the Right in the national question, the extreme internationalists Rosa Luxemburg and her many followers, Bukharin, Radek, Piatakov, and others on one side, and the 'socialist' adherents of national-cultural autonomy, the Jewish Bund and Caucasian Social Democrats on the other side. He attempts to avoid not only what he considers the pitfalls of an unrealistic super-internationalism which confuses international goals with national realities, but also the menace of a nationalism which, under the guise of realism and democracy, encroaches upon the international tasks of the socialist proletariat. He is sharply critical of the Left for ignoring national oppression, an issue closely linked with the success of the "proletarian" revolution, and of the Right for fundamental concessions to nationalism. The Left has a negative, a "nihilistic" [99] position in regard to the national question; the Right is prepared to meet nationalism half-way. Lenin shares with the Left the international outlook, while he agrees with the Right as to the actual importance of the national movement.

Neither the Left nor the Right was satisfied with Lenin's position. The numerous qualifications to national self-determination which Lenin established were not of a nature to dispel the suspicions of the Left—which held that this slogan, however restrictive the interpretation, unavoidably strengthened nationalism—while the adoption of the program of national self-determination, narrowly interpreted as the right to secession, did not pacify the Right which demanded national-cultural autonomy.[100]

Continuing his examination of Marx's position on the nationality question, Lenin draws a "conclusion" from the master's critical remarks which again makes his own views stand out sharply:

> The working class should be the last to make a fetish of the national question, since the development of capitalism does not necessarily awaken all nations to independent life. But to brush aside national mass movements once they have been started and to refuse to support what is progressive in them, means in effect pandering to nationalistic prejudices, viz. recognizing 'one's own as the model nation' (or, we will add on our part, as the nation possessing exclusive privileges of forming a state).[101]

Lenin approves what he considers Marx's policy on the national question, namely:

(1) Refusal to lend support to a national movement which has not yet "awakened" and does not appear to possess sufficient vitality to develop into a living ethnic group.

(2) Recognition of nationalism as a vital force to be taken into calculation in the struggle for socialism. Refusal to recognize it would not only reveal "nationalistic prejudice" and harm the unity of the Party, but also disregard a dynamic force, the "national mass movement."

(3) Support by the proletariat of "progressive" elements in the national movement.

Marx's policy on the nationality question seemed to Lenin to have been based upon eminently practical considerations and clearly subordinated to the primary interests of the proletariat and of socialism.

Like any strategist, Lenin refused to pin his hope on sham-battalions, on nationalities not yet awakened to national consciousness. He was resolved to count only those battalions and divisions which were ready for battle and to lend them the support of his own armies only, if the proletariat's interests were thereby furthered, if the national movement was "progressive."

Lenin draws from the position of Marx and Engels in regard to the nationality question the further conclusion that first

> the interests of the liberation of a few large and of the largest peoples of Europe must count more than the interests of the liberation movement of the small nationalities

and, secondly,

> that the demand of democracy must be considered in European scope—one must now say, from the world viewpoint—and not isolated.[102]

Engels is quoted against the "senselessness" of the principle of nationality that means to maintain the equal importance of small and large nationalities. According to Lenin, in the period of the proletarian struggle against capitalism, a situation could well arise in which the interests of the liberation movement of one nationality would clash with the interests of democracy, of the proletariat, and of socialism. It would then have to be sacrificed on the altar of these larger objectives.

Lenin's claim that Bolshevism demanded and practiced equality of all nationalities was thus in reality also vitiated by tactical considerations.[103] Repeatedly Lenin stated that the bourgeoisie of the oppressor nationality was the main foe, "the chief enemy," and, vice versa, that the interests of the proletariat of a large nation counted more heavily than those of the working class of a small nationality. If sacrifices—at times perhaps only of a temporary nature, at other times of a permanent character—had to be made, the smaller nationalities were to make them![104] Theory and practice, claim and policy, were here at loggerheads!

In the same vein Lenin disputed Karl Radek when the latter asserted that the program of self-determination obligated "Social Democrats to support every war of independence." [105]

> We are not obliged to support every movement for independence or every republican or anti-clerical movement.

> For instance, to approve a European war only and merely for the sake of the reestablishment of Poland would mean to be a nationalist of the worst kind, to put the interests of a small number of Poles higher than the interests of millions of human beings who suffer on account of the war.[106]

The interests of the democracy of one country must be subordinated to the interests of the democracy of many countries. Sometimes Social Democrats might also have to oppose the substitution of a republic for a monarchy, though, in general, they favored republicanism over monarchism. Republicanism had no absolute value, it was only one of the demands of political democracy, and as such

> subordinated to the interest of democracy in its entirety (and in even much greater measure, of course, to the interests of the socialist proletariat).[107]

The latter's interests do not "coincide" with the interests of bourgeois-capitalist democracy, though they might run parallel for some time.[108]

The program of political democracy includes national self-determination, republicanism, etc. In the capitalist era the proletariat, in general, will support demands of political democracy and also national self-determination. Yet the struggle for democratic demands must be subordinated to the revolutionary struggle for the overthrow of the bourgeoisie.[109] The interests of the proletariat and of socialism are always paramount, and support for the idea of national self-determination and of its champion, the bourgeoisie of the oppressed nationalities, is "only conditional"[110] and temporary. It is not merely given for the sake of abstract principles, "democratization," "equal national rights," "national peace," etc., but "for the sake of creating better conditions for the class struggle."[111]

To some extent, it is admitted, the proletariat supports the bourgeois nationalism of the oppressed nations, as Rosa Luxemburg had charged. Yet the proletariat's policy never "coincides" with that of the bourgeoisie of the oppressed nationalities. Rosa Luxemburg herself had completely overlooked, had "forgotten the nationalism of the Great Russians, although this latter nationalism is the most formidable at the present time." [112] While she charged that the Party's position on self-determination aided the bourgeoisie of the oppressed nationalities, her own position was giving comfort to Great Russian chauvinism.

In the later, the imperialist, phase of capitalist development, the bourgeoisie of the oppressor nation appears increasingly opposed to recognizing the right of the oppressed nations to self-determination.[113]

> Capitalism, formerly a liberator of nations, has now, in its imperialist stage, become the greatest oppressor of nations. Formerly progressive, it has become a reactionary force.[114]

The proletariat and the Social Democracy have to distinguish between the different stages of the national movement and the different roles of the bourgeoisie in connection with it. They must correspondingly also differentiate between national and imperialist wars. This distinction becomes of course especially important with the outbreak of the First World War, the great imperialist struggle.

The imperialist war is a war fought either for the maintenance of an empire, for the continued domination and exploitation of other nationalities, or for the purpose of subjecting still free nations to alien domination. A national war, however, is one fought to ward off foreign domination, or to struggle for national liberation and for the formation of an independent national state, whether in Europe or in the colonies. Lenin often declares the formation of a national state in the bourgeois stage to be "normal." [115] Likewise, he considers the uprising of an oppressed nationality for the purpose of establishing an independent state a national war and generally justifies it on this ground.

Lenin was neither opposed to war as such nor to the use of force in general. The "war" of the proletariat against the ruling class was a legitimate war. Likewise, a war for "national defense" was for "just" purposes, "legitimate" and "progressive," in the interest of the proletariat and of socialism, and therefore, in general,[116] to be supported by the Social Democratic Party. On this basis Lenin criticized Polish socialists who rejected the concept of defense of the fatherland under all circumstances.[117] "If we reject support for an uprising of the annexed regions," Lenin warned in his polemics with the Polish socialists, "we shall become, objectively, annexationists ourselves." He took the Polish comrades to task because they, though proclaiming the liberation of colonies, pleaded for "non-annulment of annexations in Europe."[118] He considered support for the uprising of oppressed nationalities not only a matter of principle, but a policy dictated by the military strategy of the revolution.

> Without abandoning socialism, we *must* support *every* uprising against our chief enemy, the bourgeoisie of the great powers, unless it is a rebellion for a reactionary class . . . It is just now in the era of imperialism, the era of the beginning social revolution, that the proletariat will support with special vigor the uprising of the annexed regions in order to attack to-morrow the bourgeoisie of a large power.[119]

The era of imperialism, one of "intensification"[120] of national oppression, was bound to produce tremendous national grievances and national uprisings. Such an age required of Social Democrats "increased utilization of all conflicts," including those of a national character, "for mass actions and revolutionary struggles against the bourgeoisie." The national liberation movement had, after all, the same chief opponent as the proletariat of the oppressor nationality, namely the bourgeoisie and possibly other allied ruling groups of the large powers.

Refusing support for the national uprisings meant rejecting the principle of national self-determination. Not to recognize the right to self-determination of the oppressed nationalities—though it might lead to the separation of some of them—would have been utterly unrealistic from Lenin's viewpoint. It would have meant to deprive the proletariat of a potential ally in the form of the national movements of the oppressed nationalities.[121] Lack of a positive national program on the part of the Bolsheviks, Lenin was convinced, would only play into the hands of the imperialist "robber" states. The division of nations into oppressor and oppressed nationalities must therefore be made one of the focal points of the Social Democratic program.[122]

With the approach and especially the outbreak of the First World War, Lenin's emphasis in his discussion of the nationality problem shifts from the more internal, specifically Russian, aspects of the national question to its international ones. Lenin's nationality program, while first clearly designed for Russia, is soon recognized as holding general significance. The nationality problem has for Lenin not only internal, but European, even world-wide implications. The struggle against the bourgeoisie of the great powers must be waged by the proletariat of the dominant nationalities, but in alliance with the national movement of the oppressed and politically ambitious peoples in Europe and in the overseas colonies.[123] The difference in the cultural and economic development between the oppressed nationalities in Europe and those in the colonies was considerable, but the role of either as ally[124] of the proletariat of the dominant nationalities in the struggle against the bourgeoisie of the imperialist nations was basically the same. Lenin's vision embraced equally Europe, Asia, Africa, the world; he abandoned the traditional and limiting view which sharply distinguished between oppressed peoples in Europe and those overseas.[125]

Theoretically, the Bolsheviks opposed annexation, a policy which was the logical outgrowth of their concept of national self-determination. Social Democrats, Lenin stressed, were not

opposed to annexation because it involved past or present application of force and, in the latter case, constituted a challenge
to the status quo. They were opposed to it because it was a
"violation of the right of a nationality to self-determination,"
because it constituted a "determination of state boundaries
against the will of the population." [126]

Karl Radek formulated the position of the Bolshevik Party
on annexation in the spirit of Lenin's pronouncements when he
spoke out "against old and new annexations." New annexations,
according to Lenin, violated the nationality's right to self-determination. Old annexations constituted old wrongs and had to
be righted by reestablishing the right of the oppressed nationality
to self-determination. Lenin sharply criticized Polish socialists
on account of what appeared to him their essentially vague assurance that they "were against annexations." [127] He approved,
conditionally, a war in defense of the fatherland against an
aggressive imperialism as well as a "just" war of liberation against
established imperialist powers.

The refusal of the Left in the Party to grant national
minorities the right to national self-determination and, correspondingly, to annul annexation and dissolve unions brought
about by force—a position which Lenin bitterly and consistently
attacked—was based upon the conviction of the great advantages
of the large economic realm and of the progressive character of
the large state. Yet Lenin branded the "refusal to consider the
question of state boundaries" as "imperialist economism," [128] a
kind of proletarian imperialism pleading economic necessity.
The fighting proletariat as well as the victorious working
class, Lenin held, cannot "reject *democratic means* of determining the boundaries of a state," cannot "refuse to take the
'sympathies' of the population into consideration." [129] The proletariat "cannot evade the question . . . of the frontiers of
states that are based on national oppression." [130] It must speak
out "against the forcible retention of the oppressed nations
within boundaries of a given state."

In the struggle for power the proletariat and the Party are, according to Lenin, not to neglect the force of nationalism. Lenin propagated the slogan of national self-determination by means of which he expected the Party to win the trust and friendship of the oppressed nationalities. But Lenin always maintained the primacy of socialism and of proletarian interests. If conflicting with these interests, those of national liberation had always to be subordinated to the struggle for socialism. Likewise, the interests of the national liberation of a small nationality had, if circumstances forced making a choice, to be sacrificed for the sake of the liberation of a major nationality. The Party reserved itself the right to refuse support to one or the other nationality.

While, in general, the Party was to support the national bourgeoisie in its struggle for liberation, the proletariat's interest and that of the "progressive" national bourgeoisie did not coincide. The support the Party was to give to a national war for liberation was always conditional. On the other hand, it always opposed an imperialist war. The proletariat and the Party were to reject the moral and legal validity equally of recent or long past annexations and, in general, to insist upon the right of all nationalities to self-determination. The proletariat and the Party, ordinarily, had to take into consideration the "sympathies" of the nationality. An "economic imperialism" which, under the guise of general welfare, disregarded their wishes as to independent states and to frontiers was considered a denial of both democracy and socialism.

In his evaluation of the historic significance of the slogan of national self-determination for the fighting proletariat Trotsky points to the circumstance that the Great Russian proletariat gained thereby the "confidence" [131] of the non-Great-Russian nationalities. Such "confidence" and trust were indeed imperative, if the proletariat was to gain allies among the oppressed nationalities. The significance of the slogan was thus largely tactical.[132]

CHAPTER FOUR

Nationality Policy During the "Proletarian" Revolution

THE SEIZURE OF POWER AND THE OPPRESSED NATIONALITIES

The Bolshevik program of national self-determination is closely linked with the "proletarian" revolution. It has been devised to speed its coming. The adoption of the slogan of self-determination is, according to Lenin, a tactical imperative: it is going to make allies of the proletariat and of broad groups among the oppressed nationalities in their struggle against imperialism. This alliance, Lenin holds, will ensure the success of the "proletarian" revolution.

Which historic circumstances make possible the collaboration, the alliance, between the proletariat and the oppressed nationalities?

Capitalism had developed unevenly in different countries, and some states were economically backward. The latter had fallen under the control of more advanced and powerful states. Characteristic for the stage of imperialism was the coexistence, side by side, of states of different economic level and political status, of oppressor nations and oppressed nationalities. The social revolution, Lenin stressed, "cannot be the united action of the proletariat of *all* countries," for the simple reason that the majority of states and the majority of the peoples of the earth are "not *in* the capitalist stage of development, but rather they have just reached it." [1]

Socialism will be effected by the proletariat of only "a minority of states," those "which have reached the stage of

⸝ment of advanced capitalism." These advanced countries —"England, France, Germany, and others"—happen to be the very ones in which the nationality question has already been "long solved" and in which, objectively, there were no longer any "general-national tasks."

The nationality problem, however, was very alive in the undeveloped states, "in the entire East of Europe" and in all colonies and "semi-colonies":

> Here, as a rule, are *still* oppressed and capitalistically un-developed nationalities . . . Among such nations there are still *objectively* general-national tasks, namely *democratic* tasks, the tasks of the overthrow of alien domination.[2]

While the proletariat of the advanced countries will over-throw the rule of the bourgeoisie and ward off its counterrevolu-tionary attempts, the undeveloped and oppressed nationalities will not stand by idly.[3] They will take advantage of the revolution and civil war in the advanced countries and stage uprisings to achieve their objectives. The rising of the oppressed nationalities during the "proletarian" revolution, during the civil war between the proletariat and the bourgeoisie of the advanced countries, will take place not merely in the colonies, but also in Europe.[4]

While at times the "proletarian" revolution is believed likely to spark the struggle for national liberation, at other times it is held that the national struggle may trigger the "socialist" revolution. This revolution

> may break out, not only in consequence of a great strike, a street demonstration, a hunger riot, a mutiny in the forces, or a *colonial* rebellion, but also in consequence of any political crisis, like the Dreyfus affair, the Zabern incident, or in connection with a *referendum on the secession of an oppressed nation,* etc.[5]

The "proletarian" revolution in economically more devel-oped countries, as well as in Russia, and the uprising of the oppressed nationalities in overseas colonies and in multinational states in Europe are directed against the same opponent, the ruling classes of the highly developed West European capitalist countries, as well as of the dominant Great Russian people. While the proletariat of the oppressor nations and the "progressive" national liberation movement have ultimately different objectives, in the immediate future they have rather common interests and a common goal, namely the defeat of the bourgeoisie of the oppressor nation.

The uneven economic and social development of different peoples and regions tended in one respect to delay the "proletarian" revolution by depriving the proletariat of the developed countries of the help of the working class of less advanced areas. On the other hand, it gave the proletariat an unexpected ally in the national liberation movements of politically dependent and economically often less developed countries. Uneven economic development of capitalism was, as far as the fighting proletariat was concerned, a hindrance in some ways, a help in others.

At times Lenin goes even so far as to make the success of the "proletarian" revolution contingent on the simultaneous uprising of the "oppressed nationalities":

> The social revolution cannot come about except in . . . an era which links the civil war of the proletariat against the bourgeoisie with a *whole series* of democratic and revolutionary movements of the less developed, backward and oppressed nationalities, among them also of national liberation movements.[6]

It was theoretically false to maintain

> that the social revolution is possible without uprisings of small nations in the colonies and in Europe.[7]

In its struggle for power the proletariat could not refuse support from any quarter. Also,

he who expects a 'pure' social revolution, will never live to
see it. He is a revolutionary only in words who does not
understand the real revolution.

The social revolution will be accompanied by

revolutionary outbreaks of a part of the petty bourgeoisie
with all its prejudices, by the movement of backward proletarians and semi-proletarian masses against the yoke of the
landowner and of the church, against monarchist and national oppression. The Russian revolution of 1905 was a
bourgeois-democratic revolution, but consisted of a series of
struggles of *all* dissatisfied classes, groups and elements of
the population.[8]

The "bourgeois-democratic" revolution of 1905 was no "pure"
revolution. The social revolution, it was Lenin's view, will likely
not be a "pure" revolution either, but a struggle of "all dissatisfied" elements of the population, including the oppressed nationalities.

Lenin stresses thus the importance of the struggle of the
oppressed nationalities against imperialist capitalism everywhere,
in the colonies and in Europe, and points to its decisive impact
on the fight of the revolutionary proletariat of the advanced
countries against its bourgeoisie.

The rising of the oppressed nationalities in Europe will likely
be of even greater assistance to the proletariat in its struggle for
power than a rebellion in a "distant colony." [9] A blow struck in
Europe is also more likely. The "dependent nations" in Europe
are economically much more developed than those in Asia—
though Lenin excepts the Albanians as well as some of the "alien
peoples of Russia." [10] The more advanced stage of Europe's
oppressed nationalities accounts for their stronger resistance to
national subjection. Revolutionary uprisings of all kinds are
in Europe "more determined, harder to quell than in the
colonies." [11]

A rising of the oppressed nationalities in Europe would deepen the revolutionary crisis more than even a widespread rebellion in the colonies.

A blow of equal strength which is administered against the power of the English imperialistic bourgeoisie by an uprising in Ireland, has a political significance a hundred times greater than an equal blow in Asia or in Africa.[12]

As an "independent factor" in the struggle against imperialism the small nationalities are "powerless." Yet it is in accordance with the "dialectics of history" that they play the role of one of the "ferments," "one of the germs" which may bring about a great transformation and may help the "true" opponent of imperialism, the socialist proletariat.

Lenin, an admirer of Clausewitz,* looked upon political warfare as a military struggle. "The general staffs in the present war," he wrote:

are intent on taking advantage of every national and revolutionary movement in the enemy's camp, the Germans— of the Irish rebellion, the French—of the Czech movement, etc. And they act correctly from their standpoint.

One cannot earnestly fight a war without exploiting the "slightest weakness" of the enemy.

We would be very poor revolutionaries indeed, if we would not know how to utilize in the great war of liberation of the proletariat for socialism *every* popular movement against . . . imperialism.[13]

This is indeed a frank statement. Yet, if the much propagandized right to self-determination was primarily a slogan and had essentially tactical significance, was Lenin's much publicized program for the solution of the nationality question an honest one? Did he truly believe that national self-determination would

---

* Noted German theoretician of military strategy.

solve the national question in the stages of the proletarian state
and of socialism? Was he genuinely interested in a solution of
the nationality problem? Or was he, certainly not "a poor revolutionary," but rather a good one, primarily bent on exploiting
its revolutionary potentialities prior to and during the "proletarian" revolution?

How substantial was the right to secession during the stages
of the "proletarian" revolution, of the "proletarian" state, and
of socialism? Did Lenin himself consider secession in these stages
advisable from the point of view of the interests of the proletariat and the broad masses of the border nationalities? Were
all the numerous nationalities of Russia actually then to possess
this right or were some denied it outright? And if so, why? Was
the right to self-determination a genuine one, to be granted
immediately after the seizure of power by the Great Russian
"proletariat," the proletariat of the dominant nationality? Was
it to be a permanent right of the nationalities? Was it to be
exercised by the entire population of the border nationality or
merely by its proletariat? And, last but not least, was the govern-
ing Party to bow to an adverse decision of the border nationality
or the border proletariat?

An attempt will be made in the following to give answers
to these vital questions—questions which, strangely, perhaps un-
derstandably enough, Lenin never openly raised.

The Right to Secession. Advisability and Limitations

The large state, Lenin pointed out repeatedly, was preferable
for the proletariat, not only in the bourgeois-capitalist stage, but
also in the stages of proletarian dictatorship and socialism. The
large state offered its inhabitants great economic advantages
in either stage.

A large state under socialism will mean so many hours of
work less every day and so much more earnings every day

. . . Liberated from the yoke of the bourgeoisie, the masses of the toilers will strive with all their might to ally themselves with the great advanced socialist nations.[14]

They will do so not for the sake of any "cultural aid," but for the sake of concrete economic advantages,[15] provided only

that the former oppressors do not offend the highly developed democratic sense of self-respect of the long oppressed nations, that they only grant them equality in everything.[16]

The Party's nationality policy during the period of "proletarian" dictatorship must strengthen the natural economic trend toward the development of the large state. It also ought to discourage cultural "insularity" and national "narrowmindedness" [17] which went hand in hand with a small state. For economic and cultural reasons the Party must attempt to maintain the larger realm of the multinational state.

Under capitalism the multinational state is considered a backward state.[18] Under the proletarian dictatorship and under socialism the multinational state has apparently lost this character. The multinational state is the larger state, and the larger state, other conditions being equal, is to be preferred by the fighting and by the victorious proletariat.

While, in general, Lenin clings to the widely propagandized right of all nationalities to self-determination, he entertains the hope that the Party's policy before and during the "proletarian" revolution, coupled with the apparent economic advantages of the large state, is going to turn any hesitating nationality back to the multinational state, even though it had formerly been an object of fear and hate. Lenin's preference is clearly for the large multinational state. The large realm is in conformity with the demands of economy and of internationalism.

The fight against nationalism and for internationalism in the ranks of the struggling as well as of the victorious proletariat takes, according to Lenin, different forms, depending on whether the proletariat concerned is that of the oppressor or of the oppressed nationality. Both must place the interests of "all nations" above the interests of their own nationality. Great Russian workers must realize that it is their duty to grant self-determination to Polish workers. The Great Russian and German worker is duty-bound to support the free separation of the Poles. Otherwise he would be nothing but a lackey of Nicholas II or of Hindenburg.[19] The Social Democrats of the oppressor nations must be true internationalists, must fight imperialism and narrow nationalism, and must insist on "freedom of separation" on the part of the oppressed peoples.[20]

The Social Democrats of the oppressed nationalities, on the other hand, must demand "freedom of union." [21] It is the duty of the socialists of the oppressed nationalities to work toward preserving the multinational state by stressing the "right to union" and to strive for the reconciliation among the various nationalities and toward "amalgamation." The proletariat, irrespective of its particular national situation and its peculiar national problems, must under all circumstances fight for international goals:

A Social Democrat belonging to a small nation must place the weight of his agitation on the *second* word in our general formula 'voluntary amalgamation' of nations. He may, without violating his duties as an internationalist, be in favor *either* of the political independence of his nation *or* of its inclusion in neighboring states, X, Y, Z, etc. But in all cases he must fight *against* small-nation narrowmindedness, insularity and aloofness, he must fight for the recognition of the whole and the general and for the subordination of the interests of the particular to the interests of the general.[22]

Lenin acknowledges that a Social Democrat of a small nationality—the latter not necessarily, but often, especially in Russia, identical with an oppressed people—may be an internationalist in spite of his favoring political independence for his national group. Yet the whole emphasis of the foregoing quotation, and of numerous others, lies rather in the opposite direction. How indeed can "political independence" and voluntary "amalgamation" be reconciled? True independence did not have to lead to amalgamation at all. Was "amalgamation" only cultural and economic and not also political? Would the continued existence, side by side, of two proletarian states, in both of which proletarian dictatorship had been established, not be subject to criticism on the basis of the above remarks, on account of "small-nation narrowmindedness, insularity, and aloofness" of the proletariat and the Social Democratic Party of the smaller nationality which continued to resist political "amalgamation"?

The right to secession, proclaimed by the proletariat of the oppressor nation, must be countered, Lenin holds, with the right to "free union" with the established state, proclaimed by the proletariat of the oppressed nationality. In accordance with this attitude, "the socialists of the *oppressed* nations must unequivocally fight for complete unity of *workers* of both the oppressed and oppressor nationalities (which means organizational unity)." [23] Once such unity has been achieved, it is likely to support powerfully the endeavors of the proletariat of the border nationality for "union" with the multinational state. The right to secession and the right to "free union"—this is Lenin's two-headed formula of national self-determination which alone, in his opinion, ensured unitary action on the part of the proletariat and of the Party and national harmony among the working class.

The slogan "freedom of union" is to place propagandistic emphasis upon the right of the formerly oppressed nationality to union, a "freedom" which in the past has hardly had much appeal. Its apparent purpose is to hold before the eyes of the oppressed nationality an alternative to secession, namely continued "union," though on a more appealing basis than in the past, on terms of freedom and equality for all nationalities and of rejection of all discrimination on national or other grounds.

The seemingly centrifugal effect of the slogan of the proletariat of the oppressor nation, the right to secession, was thus to be counterbalanced by the centripetal effect of the slogan of the proletariat of the oppressed nationalities, "freedom of union."

The duty which Lenin assigns to the proletariat of the oppressed nationality, namely to proclaim the "freedom of union," opens the back door through which the Social Democratic Party of the oppressed nationality may lead its people back to the multinational state. The apparent gap between Lenin's insistence upon the right of the oppressed nationality to secession and his stress on the advantages of the large state is to be bridged by the duty of the proletariat of the oppressed nationality to insist upon the "freedom of union."

The proletariat of the oppressor nation, however, must emphasize the right to separation. It must disavow force and compulsion and insist on national equality in the new state. The "union" of all nationalities which compose it must be a free one.

Oppression of a national minority after the "proletarian" seizure of power was held to be entirely impossible:

> The victorious socialism must realize full democracy and, consequently, effect not only full equality of the nations, but also the self-determination of the oppressed nationalities.

Social Democratic Parties must prove

> that they will liberate the oppressed nationalities and will establish their own relations with them on the basis of a free union.

Otherwise, "such Parties would commit treason to socialism." [24]

Lenin's view of the necessity of a voluntary union, in contradistinction to one based upon force, and his cautious approach toward formerly oppressed nationalities emerge clearly also in his letter to Shaumian. The latter had voiced his belief that a single state language was imperative for Russia. Lenin, while admitting that the Russian language had, without doubt, been of great benefit to many backward and pitiable nationalities, added a word of warning:

> Don't you see that it would be of even greater progressive significance if no force existed?

Force would rather have a contrary, a detrimental effect.

> Why can't you understand the psychology which is especially important in the national question? . . . the application of the least force vilifies and destroys the indisputably progressive significance of centralization, of large states, of the single language.[25]

According to Lenin, the mere acknowledgment of the right to secession by the formerly oppressed nationalities on the part of the Great Russian proletariat and its renunciation of force as the means of holding together the nationalities of Russia would have a profound impact upon the non-Russian nationalities. They would thus be persuaded that the Great Russians had forever shed their notions of national superiority and their will to domination. The Party's policy, its mere declaration, will sweep away the bitterness of past oppression and the accumulated hate against yesterday's oppressor nations; it will tilt the scales in favor of unitary and integrating forces against disruptive and disintegrating tendencies.[26]

The "proletarian" revolution, repudiating any union produced by force, will bring about a unitary and centralized state. Federalism in the period under discussion is generally sharply rejected by Lenin. The state which the border nationality will join, in which it will remain, or from which it will secede, will be a centralized one.

The border nationality will have no right to demand a federal state structure[27] and will obtain none. No concessions in the form of federalism will be made to it to keep it in the new "proletarian" polyglot state. Having voluntarily joined a centralized state, the border nationality has also subsequently no right to demand a transformation toward a federal or confederate state structure.[28]

The border nationality which has cast its lot with the multinational state has, politically, committed suicide. A revival of its sovereign status is precluded. Lenin never discusses openly this aspect of his "doctrine" of nationality, but rather buries it in silence. Yet it should be clear that the strongly centralized state will never relinquish what it has absorbed as consequence of a voluntary act on the part of the border nationality. The latter has thus made an irrevocable decision. It has delivered itself, for better or worse, into the hands of the Great Russians. National self-determination, it must be concluded, is no permanent right of the national minorities.

This comes rather as an anticlimax in view of the central role which national self-determination has been assigned to play in Bolshevik nationality theory and propaganda. The right to self-determination, so much exalted by Lenin, is in some cases—whenever the nationality has resolved to remain in the multinational state—reduced to a single decision.[29] If the nationality thereafter should reach the conclusion that it has made a mistake, the regret would come too late. The error which it committed would be fatal. Lenin, of course, was convinced that a decision for the proletarian multinational state was always the correct one, in the interests of integration and proletarian unity, of socialism and internationalism, against the splitting up of states and against disintegration and nationalism.

While the national minority which has decided against separation has relinquished its short-lived sovereignty to the former oppressor nationality, without any safeguard for the future and no possibility of reversing its decision, the nationality which has voted for secession and a separate political existence retains the sovereign right to review the decision any time thereafter.[30] A later reunion would require the consent also of the former oppressor nation, but the latter is not likely to deny this consent.

The nationality which has seceded has by the very act of secession given proof of its sovereign will. Its desire for independence has reached the climax of fulfilment; subsequently, however, the nationality will face the hard economic realities of everyday life, the hardships of the reduced political and economic status of a petty state.[31] The reduction of nationalism, which has lost its most powerful stimulus with the abolishment of oppression[32] and foreign rule, and economic calculation may lead the nationality which has seceded back to the multinational state. The Bolshevik policy of self-determination will thus be vindicated.

While Lenin himself does not clearly outline such a development, it appears that he held this to be the most likely course in the case of the separation of a nationality—itself considered not very probable either before, during, or after the "proletarian" revolution.

When, after the "proletarian" seizure of power, are the border nationalities to avail themselves of the right to self-determination? Is this decision, which is to take the form either of a plebiscite or a legislative act,[33] to be made during the "proletarian" revolution, during the dictatorship of the proletariat, or during the later stages of socialism and communism?

At no time did Lenin give a clear-cut answer to this question. It appears, however, that he assumed that this first, and in some cases final, act of self-determination would generally take place during the "proletarian" revolution. In a few isolated instances the right to national self-determination may already have been exercised under capitalism and may possibly have led to secession. In these rather "exceptional" [34] cases the nationalities concerned might possibly reverse their decision. In general, however, national self-determination, like most other "democratic reforms," will be "started" "in the process of the overthrow" of capitalism. Some reforms might be commenced "after it [the overthrow] has been accomplished." [35] Some question may be raised whether Lenin meant the latter statement to apply to national self-determination. There would, however, be no reason or justification to delay the vote of the border nationalities after the "proletarian" seizure of power. The victorious proletariat could otherwise not retain the confidence and trust of the border nationalities, a trust which appears to Lenin so vital.

It was in the nature of this particular "democratic reform" —a plebiscite or a vote in the legislative assembly of the border nationality—that its "start" and its end would coincide. The vote was likely to take place "during" the process of the overthrow of capitalism, during the "proletarian" revolution. The right of national minorities to decide their future appears to have been focused into this stage.

During and after the "proletarian" revolution the proletariat of the border nationalities, whether it has seceded or not, will participate in *"state* construction";[36] this seems to exclude the stages of socialism and communism as periods during which the right to national self-determination, to secession, is to be exercised. Nationalities, however, which will secede from the multinational state during the "proletarian" revolution could presumably rejoin the multinational state also during these later stages of socialism and communism, though Lenin does not specifically say so.

In the great majority of cases, however, the border nationality was during the "proletarian" revolution likely to remain in the multinational state. This was especially to be expected, if the proletariat and the Party had gained control also of the border region. After having reached the decision to remain in the polyglot state, the border nationality was, as stated, not entitled to any further act of self-determination. Yet, was not national self-determination, the first act of which was also the last one, clearly deceit?

Lenin rejects force as the basis for a "union" of the nationalities. Yet he does not disdain taking undue advantage of the decision of a border nationality which may come to regret it. Does this not mean holding the border nationality in the multi-national state against its will? By force? How genuine would constitutional government be if the responsibility of the law-makers and of the executive to the electorate were limited to a single instance in a lifetime? How genuine is national self-determination if the nationality, without guarantees on the part of the formerly dominant nation, surrenders itself and its sovereignty in an act of blind faith or folly, denying thus the very principle of self-determination?

Thin and unsubstantial as national self-determination appears on this ground in regard to the border nationalities, it was, if possible, even more shallow in the case of the national minorities located in the interior of the country.

That a decision for separation might be nullified by plain geography must have entered Lenin's mind. The political geography of Russia was then characterized, as it is today, by a ring of border nationalities surrounding the Great Russian people. Secession under such circumstances was for many national minorities a possibility, technically speaking, but by no means for all. If geography had "discriminated" against a nationality by placing it in the interior of the country, even Lenin with his winning formula was unable to right the wrong.

For the national minorities of Russia which lived in the interior, Lenin's formula of national self-determination, narrowly conccived as right to secession—and not as right to federalism and autonomy—meant little indeed.[37] This appears to have been one of the obvious weaknesses in Lenin's nationality program. True, Lenin assured the national minorities that autonomy was the Party's program; but it was an autonomy to be granted by the central government, and not guaranteed in the constitution, and could be withdrawn any time. All that the members of nationalities situated in the interior of Russia might count on in the case of a "proletarian" revolution was Lenin's, that is, the Great Russian proletariat's promise to end all national discrimination—which was to benefit them individually—and to grant autonomy—which may have raised their hopes that they would be able to maintain and develop their national culture. Yet it was only a promise and a hope, no assurance, no constitutional guarantee. Lenin stressed that the nationalities had no "right" to autonomy, though autonomy was included in the Party's program.

Lenin left little doubt that he considered any secessionist movement during the "proletarian" revolution hardly justified from the viewpoint of proletarian and socialist interests, though he was willing to uphold the right of the border nationality to secede.

Yet self-determination, Lenin made rather clear, was not to be a permanent right of the border nationality, but was to be enjoyed and exercised only during the brief period of the "proletarian" revolution. And this right meant literally nothing in the case of a minority placed in the interior of the country.

SELF-DETERMINATION AND ITS IMPLEMENTATION. THE PROLETARIAT AND THE PARTY.

Aside from these serious limitations to the widely proclaimed right to national self-determination, there were even more far-reaching ones: in the summer of 1913 Lenin had assigned to the Party the all-important task of deciding "each individual case" of national self-determination "separately," [38] on its own merits. The highly centralistic Party was thus to play a decisive role in the implementation of national self-determination, to hold, after the seizure of power, a virtual veto over it. Under these circumstances, how genuine, how meaningful was the Bolshevik slogan of the right of all nations to self-determination?

Yet Lenin becomes rather angry if doubts are raised as to the genuineness of his program. He voices indignation at Semkovskii, who had maintained that the Party required a decision on secession by the "central parliament" instead of by a "regional plebiscite." It had not occurred to him, Lenin scolds, that the right to secession presupposed the settlement of the question

> *not* by the central parliament, but by the parliament (diet, referendum, etc.) of the seceding region. When Norway separated from Sweden (in the year 1905), Norway *alone* (which is itself half as large as Sweden) decided this.[39]

This appears definitely to exclude the "central parliament," central public authorities, from making the decision concerning the secession of the border region and to reserve this question, in accordance with an honest interpretation of self-determination, either to the regional legislative assembly or directly to the voters of the region.

There are numerous other statements of Lenin which, at first glance, make it difficult to question his sincerity and genuine belief in the desirability and, from a democratic and socialist viewpoint, necessity of national self-determination. Victorious socialism, he asserts, must also "achieve complete democracy" and

> consequently not only bring about complete equality of nations, but also give effect to the right of oppressed nations to self-determination, i.e. right to free political secession.

Anything to the contrary would be "treachery to socialism." [40]

> The right to self-determination is such that an undemocratic decision of the question of separation is impossible.[41]

Bourgeois political democracy is reconcilable, it is further held here, with an "oppressive nationalism." The proletariat, however, "demands a democracy which excludes the forcible detention of a nation within the state borders." [42]

"At the present time," Lenin continues, "reactionary, imperialist capitalism" was "often breaking down" the "democratically determined boundaries" of the epoch of "progressive capitalism in Europe," of the era of 1848-71. "Victorious socialism" will be left with "a number of annexations in Europe and in other parts of the globe" which had taken place during recent decades, "a heritage of less democratic boundaries." "Well," Lenin raises the rhetorical question,

> will victorious socialism, in restoring democracy and applying it logically all along the line, reject democratic means of determining the boundaries of a state? Will it refuse to take the 'sympathies' of the population into consideration. One has only to put these questions to see plainly that our Polish colleagues are slipping from Marxism into 'imperialist economism.' [43]

Disregard by the fighting proletariat or by "victorious socialism" of the reality of the subjection of some nationalities by others would run counter to democracy. The proletariat, however, must fight for democracy, and socialism must "restore" democracy among the different nationalities by annulling annexation. Not the "central parliament," but the regional "parliament" or the local population through a "referendum" is to decide the question of secession. This apparently forthright program of nationality would seem to justify a democratic interpretation of Lenin's concept of national self-determination.

Was, however, the regional "parliament" truly representative of the entire border nationality, of all its different social strata? Was the election of this "parliament" or the vote in the regional "referendum" based on universal suffrage or on a restricted one so as to exclude the upper and middle classes of the border nationalities? Lenin made repeated references to free and democratic elections, yet they were not reassuring since he simply did not raise these questions, and did not disclose his views on them.

Assuming that it was the proletariat of the border region and not the border nationality in its entirety which was to decide the question of secession, would such a decision be democratic?

Would it be democratic if the proletariat formed a majority of the border population? If it constituted less than a majority? Could one consider a decision in either case to be in accordance with "true self-determination" and would a union which would spring from such a decision be "voluntary"?

The Party, of course, held the key to the implementation of the nationality policy, of national self-determination, during and after the "proletarian" revolution. Yet Lenin did not clarify its precise role in this crucial task and shed little light on the relative functions of the Party as a whole, of its regional branch, and of the regional proletariat in fulfilling its promise.

The task Lenin assigns to the Party in implementing the program of national self-determination emerges from the Party Resolution of the summer of 1913 on the nationality question:

> The Social Democratic Party must decide this question [of secession] in each individual case separately, from the viewpoint of the interests of the general social development and the interests of the proletarians' class struggle for socialism.[44]

Where, however, does this leave the regional branch of the Party and the regional proletariat?

Lenin's notion of "democratic centralism," which represents his ideal of Party organization, does not permit any federalism and regional independence. The regional branch of the Party, clearly, can take no initiative in regard to national separation or, for that matter, in anything else. It is the centralistic Party which is to judge the advisability of secession in each case on the basis "of the general social development" and the general proletarian and socialist interests. Even if the regional branch of the Party possessed any initiative, as it does not, it need, first, not be truly representative of the border proletariat in regard to its national wishes and, secondly, it would likely have the proletarian "duty" to insist upon the "right to union." In implementing national self-determination, the regional Party had no independent role to play.

Which part was the regional proletariat to perform? Would the proletariat fulfill its socialist duty by proclaiming the "right to union" and linking its fortunes with the proletariat of the formerly dominant nationality? Was it certain that the proletariat, nursing perhaps past national grievances and carried away by national emotion, would recognize its true proletarian interests and cast its vote for union with the proletarian multinational state? Was the Party, the vanguard of the proletariat, to lead the regional proletariat, or was it to accept its likely different wishes in regard to its national future? Would it bow to the regional proletariat if it should insist on secession or would it impose its "better" judgment upon a recalcitrant border proletariat? Would any mere pressure, however, be reconcilable with a free and democratic decision of the border nationality? Lenin does not even pose these questions.

On the crucial problem of the implementation of self-determination Lenin was vague, evasive, and contradictory, though the incongruities and contradictions at times disclose a meaningful pattern. For instance, he was aroused by Semkovskii who interpreted the Party's position as favoring a decision on secession by the "central parliament," instead of by the "regional parliament" or by a regional "plebiscite." Yet he found the circumstance that it was the centralistic Party, and not its regional branch, which was to decide the advisability of secession "in each case" quite in order, consistent, and democratic. He rightly considered a decision on secession by the "central parliament" a travesty of self-determination. Yet on the Party level, differently from the state level, the subordination of the decision of the regional branch to that of the entire Party was paraded as democratic and as being in accordance with genuine self-determination.

Lenin once was asked point-blank the question of what the Bolsheviks would do, if the reactionaries were in control of the border nationality:

'What shall happen when the reactionaries are in the majority?' asks Mr. Semkovskii. This is one of those questions of which it is said that seven fools ask more than ten wise men can answer.[45]

Driven into a corner, Lenin tried to escape with a joke.

Earlier, at the Second Party Congress, Lenin in his "Speech on the Question of the Position of the Bund in the RSDRP"[46] had put the problem of Bolshevik nationality policy after the "proletarian" seizure of power on a different plane, that of proletarian "duty." "Struggle for complete equality" and "even[!] for the recognition of the self-determination of the peoples" was "a duty of our entire Party."

> If therefore any part of our Party should not fulfill this duty, it would on the basis of our principles unconditionally have to be condemned, it would call forth a rectification through the central agencies of the Party.[47]

Yet if "any part" of the Party had a material stake in denying to border nationalities the right to self-determination, it was most likely the "central agencies of the Party" themselves in which the Great Russian element was likely to prevail. As if Lenin had anticipated this objection, he had added:

> And when this duty ["of recognizing the right to self-determination"] was knowingly and deliberately not fulfilled, . . . such a violation of duty would signify *treason*.[48]

Yet who was to raise the charge of "treason" against "central agencies of the Party," the only bodies which could possibly commit this crime? The only guarantee that the Party would live up to its apparently noble and generous nationality program was, Lenin seemed to assure, its ideological honesty and integrity. The Party as such could be relied upon not to commit "treason." Yet while Lenin could be solemnly earnest about the nationality policy of the Bolshevik Party and indignantly reject any doubt of its integrity, he could also joke that "seven fools ask more than ten wise men can answer."

Lenin could hardly wish that the Party grant national minorities freedom of separation under all circumstances, even if bourgeois or feudal elements were in political control of the border regions. He could hardly hold that under such political and social conditions the "referendum" of which he spoke was a true expression of the national will of the border peoples. Was he not bound to look upon secessionists as "reactionary," "provincial," and "narrow-minded"? Would not separation, after the "proletarian" revolution, run counter to the interests of the proletariat and of socialism? Had not Lenin definitely subordinated the fulfillment of a democratic demand, like self-determination of the one or the other nationality, to the interests of international democracy in general, also to those of a large nationality, and to the interests of the proletariat and of socialism? And was the Party not the guardian of proletarian and socialist interests? To raise these questions is equivalent to answering them.

That Lenin was fully and keenly aware of the impact of the organizational structure of the Party on the ultimate decision of secession during the "proletarian" revolution emerges from his comment on the program of the Austrian Social Democracy. The latter, though it did not specifically include the right to national self-determination in its program, was, in Lenin's opinion, "nevertheless quite reconciled to the demand for national independence" being put forward

by *sections* of the Party. In reality, this means, of course, recognition of the right of nations to self-determination.[49]

Since the structure of the Austrian Social Democratic Party was a federal one, the Austrian Social Democracy was in Lenin's view "reconciled" to the program of national self-determination, though it was not spelled out in the Party program. In the Bolshevik program, self-determination was not only distinctly spelled out, but it was even shouted from the roof tops. Yet the Party was a strictly unitary Party, and this circumstance was quite reassuring to Lenin. He made certain that the question of secession was to be decided by the unitary, centralistic Party and not put forward by any regional-national "section."

Federalism in the Party would make possible real independence of the regional "section" and thus secession of the border nationality at the opportune moment. A unitary and centralistic structure of the Party, while not making secession actually impossible, would make it less likely, leaving the decision as to the probable impact of the separation of a nationality upon the "interests of the general social development" not to the regional branch of the Party, but to the latter itself.

There was clearly a conflict between the principle of democratic centralism,[50] at the very center of Bolshevik thought on organization in general, and national self-determination, the core of Lenin's and of the Bolsheviks' nationality program. The first-named principle, exalted by Lenin, did not permit the making of vital decisions on the periphery, by the regional "sections" of the Party or by the proletariat of the border nationality. National self-determination, on the other hand, if it was to have any meaning at all, demanded categorically a free regional decision. In the struggle of these two principles, genuine democracy was not on the side of "democratic centralism"; democracy rather sided here entirely with the region which decided freely its fate, in accordance with national self-determination. Lenin appears to have been well aware of the conflict of these two principles. In a letter to Shaumian he wrote in 1913:

> The right to self-determination is an *exception* from our general premise of centralism. This exception is absolutely necessary in view of the arch-reactionary Great Russian nationalism.

Generally, "separation is by no means our plan." [51]

Lenin, it appears, was willing to make an "exception" to the principle of "democratic centralism." He exalted this "exception" to be a principle itself, because it was bound to be tactically most useful. Yet the foregoing quotation reveals Lenin's reluctance and uneasiness; he does not want to be compelled to make this exception to "democratic centralism." Thus he qualifies self-determination, first theoretically, and then practically. He qualifies the "exception" to "our general premise of centralism"; he makes exceptions to the "exception." We have noticed before some of these theoretical qualifications to national self-determination.[52] The foregoing Party Resolution of 1913 establishes, in addition, practical exceptions by reserving to the Party the authority to "decide" "each case" of national self-determination "separately." The Bolshevik Party gave life to national self-determination only to kill the infant. Self-determination was indeed rather short-lived. By making the unitary, centralistic Party, by its very nature hostile to separation and independence of any sort, the ultimate judge of the advisability of secession in "each case," true national self-determination departs from the scene and "democratic centralism" makes a triumphant return.

Was not the program of national self-determination under these circumstances a mere fraud and hypocrisy? Lenin was hardly above resorting to hypocrisy, if the interests of the proletariat, of proletarian dictatorship, and ultimately of socialism were involved. Yet, could he permit fraud and hypocrisy if he thereby ran the risk of defeating his own purposes? Of undermining the confidence of the proletariat of the oppressed nationalities in regard to the honesty and true internationalism of the working class of the oppressor nationalities? The whole purpose of the slogan of national self-determination was to persuade the oppressed nationalities and their working classes of the honesty and the fair dealing of the Great Russian proletariat and its Social Democratic Party, and to create "mutual confidence" and "class solidarity" [53] among the proletarians of the different nationalities which inhabited the polyglot empire.

Could it be expected that Lenin's highly centralized Party, having seized power, would permit secession of a border nationality? Though this was not likely as a rule, the possibility of such a decision in one or the other case was apparently seriously considered by Lenin. Its propaganda value would possibly outweigh any temporary loss.

A "plebiscite" either could be granted by the ruling Party to the border nationality or it could be denied. In the first case, the Party still remained interested in the reaffirmation of the multinational state by the border proletariat or the border nationality in its entirety, and not in secession, though by permitting the plebiscite it had assumed the risk of an unfavorable decision. While granting a plebiscite, the Party and its regional branch were not committed to abstaining from a political campaign against secession.

Permitting to one or the other border nationality a "plebiscite," granting to it the right to self-determination, in accordance with its much publicized nationality policy, was a concession by the ruling Party, a concession which was politically motivated. If the plebiscite was to lead to actual secession, the Party could, of course, continue to work for reconsideration of the issue, for a reversal of the decision.

It is most likely that Lenin's thought moved then along these lines and that he wished the Party to accept an adverse decision of one or the other border nationality, especially since he expected it to be a rather rare phenomenon, and also only a temporary one. In any case, in his position on the nationality question Lenin is motivated less by democracy or moral indignation—though his writings give at times the impression of both—but by cold, calculating pragmatism. He also makes it amply clear that he opposes union by force because he doubts its effectiveness.

Pragmatism appears to be the key to solve the "riddle" of the Bolshevik doctrine of national self-determination. The tacti-

cal usefulness of the right to national self-determination is held
to be so great as to justify the shelving—often only temporary—
of many a vaunted Bolshevik principle.

The decision of the Party on any aspect of the nationality
question depends, according to Lenin, on the concrete situation
in Russia and in the border regions in particular and on the
international situation in general. "A thousand factors," Lenin
maintains,

> which cannot be foreseen, will determine whether the
> Ukraine, for example, is destined to form an independent
> state. . . . Without attempting idle 'guesses'

the proletariat must uphold "the right of the Ukraine to form
such a state." [54] Lenin's pragmatic approach to the national
question is always evident. He holds it impossible to

> estimate beforehand all the possible correlations between
> the bourgeois emancipation movements of the oppressed
> nations and the proletarian emancipation movement of the
> oppressing nation.[55]

In spite of the recognition of the right to national self-determination in general, each claim to secession is to be examined
by the proletariat and the Party individually, on its own merits,
namely on the basis of whether or not a separation would be
in the interest of the proletariat. In a letter to N. D. Kiknadze of
October 16, 1913, Lenin wrote:

> We are not opposed to national rebellion, but in favor of it.
> This is clear. We cannot go any further. We shall examine
> each case separately.[56]

Lenin refuses to tie the proletariat's and the Party's hands in
advance, to say, before any nationality raises the demand for
secession, "a plain 'yes' in favor of the separation of *this or that*
nation." [57]

No general political formula applicable to all nationalities, places, times, and conditions could possibly be given, nor was intended to be given by Lenin. The foremost rule observed by a shrewd tactician would be not to become entangled in his own tactical formula. It appears that while Lenin indicated the broad outlines of his nationality policy, he first held it hardly advisable politically to paint it to the last detail and, secondly, impossible to do so.

Lenin held it necessary that during the "proletarian" revolution the Party grant self-determination to some nationalities and refuse it to others.[58] Though he liked to accuse his opponents of opportunism,[59] his was an opportunism unabashed,[60] and he raised it to the level of a policy. He no doubt was willing to give what no longer could be withheld and to withhold what none could yet take. Here probably lies the "secret" of Lenin's numerous qualifications, of his omissions and contradictions, in short of the lack of clarity in regard to his nationality theory and policy.

Lenin's "opportunism" reveals itself even in his thinking on the problem of federalism and nationality, though he is more consistent in this aspect of his nationality theory than in others. He is sharply opposed to federalism and accepts it only in "exceptional" cases for the "proletarian" state.

Federalism and Autonomy

Prior to 1917 Lenin did not hold federalism to be compatible with the interests of the working class at any stage, whether under capitalism, under the dictatorship of the proletariat, or under socialism. He rejected federalism—a "Philistine ideal" [61]—for all stages of social development as a pattern both for the structure of the Social Democratic Party *and* of the state.

The organizational ideal that Lenin had evolved for the Party—a tight, centralistic structure—he also adopted for the state. A strongly centralized Party seemed to him a prerequisite of victory over Tsarism, "necessary" for the "successful struggle"

against the "autocracy." [62] Federalism, including federalism
based on national grounds, was "harmful," because it tended to
perpetuate distrust and "alienation" among workers of different
nationalities,[63]

> because it legalizes . . . separation and alienation, raises
> it to be a principle, a law.[64]

As Lenin rejects federation for the Party, he rejects it also
for the state, especially the proletarian state. "It is not the task
of the proletariat to propagate federalism." [65] Only "in a few
exceptional cases" may the Party come forth with a demand for
"the substitution of the complete political unity of a state by
a looser federal unity," and "strongly support it." [66] At the most,
federalism, Lenin points out, could be defended as an exception,
but never as a rule. And as such it was to be limited to the
state and not to extend to the Party; the latter was always to
retain its centralistic structure.

What was Lenin's conception of the correlation between
national self-determination and federalism? In his correspondence with Lenin, Shaumian, interpreting self-determination in
a broader sense of the word, held that it included not merely
the right to separation, but also the right to federalism and the
right to autonomy. Though Lenin soon thereafter was openly
to admit that, "speaking in the abstract," both federalism and
autonomy "fall under self-determination," [67] in his reply to
Shaumian he denied that self-determination embraced the right
to federalism. "Federalism," he asserted,

> is an alliance of equals, an alliance which needs a *general*
> agreement. How can there be a *right* of *one* side to the
> *consent* of the other side? This is absurd. We are in prin-
> ciple against federalism; the latter weakens economic *inte-*
> *gration,* it is a type of government irreconcilable with a
> *unitary state.*[68]

Lenin, speaking here for the Great Russian proletariat, was unwilling to give the consent of the Great Russians, of the "other side."

> Do you want to separate yourself? Then, please, do not decide in my name, don't believe, you had a 'right' to federalism.[69]

Lenin is for the "unitary state." Federalism, he asserted, "weakens economic integration." Another time he held that federalism was a "step towards splitting of nations." [70] The national minority could secede; should it, however, decide to remain in the multinational state, it would have to abandon any thought of federalism. It had no "right" to demand a federal structure in the multinational state, and the Great Russian nationality was not obligated to concede federalism to it. While maintaining that the Great Russian nation, certainly an "equal" of the minority people, as he piously asserted, had the right to reject the federal bond, he assumed that the border nationality would be unable to sever the existing economic ties. Secession would entail serious economic difficulties for the new nationality; fear of such dire consequences might dissuade the border nationality from seceding from the established multinational state. "Go to the devil," he wrote to S. G. Shaumian on December 6, 1913, in reference to the oppressed nationality, "if you [the nationality] can tear asunder the economic ties!" [71] Lenin counted thus on the economic inferiority, on the economic dependence of the border nationality.

The national minority had an inherent right neither to federalism nor to "autonomy":

> The recognition of the 'right of nations to autonomy' is as absurd as the 'right of nations to federation.' [72]

Yet Lenin assured all concerned that autonomy was "our plan for the construction of a democratic state." After the "proletarian" revolution the working class would grant autonomy to territorial nationalities as well as to other distinct groups. The

Great Russian proletariat was opposed to federalism, but not to autonomy. But neither the border nationality nor any other nationality located in the interior of the country had a *right* to either federalism or autonomy.[73]

In a project for the platform of the Fourth Congress of the Social Democratic Party of Latvia, Lenin demanded "far-reaching self-administration and autonomy of the individual regions the borders of which are to be established on the basis of ethnic criteria." [74] In granting autonomy and drawing the borders of the autonomous regions, the proletarian dictatorship would be guided by the criterion of nationality.

Yet, in view of the absence of a federal state structure, there was no guarantee that the proletarian dictatorship would not at some future date introduce other than ethnic, for instance, economic criteria in setting up new autonomous regions or changing the boundaries of old ones. The border nationality which in accordance with the principle of national self-determination had decided to throw in its lot with the multinational state had thereby once and for all relinquished the right of being treated in the future as a distinct, indestructible unit, entitled to autonomy within permanent ethnic-regional boundaries. The border nationality had deprived itself of the right to perpetuate and develop its distinct national culture.[75]

In his letter to Shaumian, Lenin made reference to the former's distinction between autonomy and "self-administration": Shaumian did not clarify these terms and did not establish the difference between them. He accepted "self-administration," but expressed fear of and opposition to autonomy. Lenin, while admitting his opposition to federalism, tried to persuade his correspondent that fear of autonomy in Russia was "ridiculous":

> Think of the explanation of Engels that centralism did by no means exclude the local 'freedoms.' Why autonomy for the Poles, but not for the Caucasus, the South, the Ural? The *borders* of autonomy are after all determined by the central parliament.[76]

The "central parliament" would determine the "borders of autonomy"—here understood as legal boundaries rather than geographic ones—but the central parliament's jurisdiction comprised also the determination of the latter. Federalism was irreconcilable with, was the very opposite to, the almost unlimited power of the "central parliament," and was therefore rejected by Lenin. Autonomy, however, left the ultimate power with the "central parliament," and was for this reason acceptable to him.

The explanation for Lenin's rejection of federalism and approval of autonomy lies in the Bolshevik conception of "democratic centralism." [77] This concept applied not merely to the structure of the Party,[78] but also to that of the state after the "proletarian" revolution. In accordance with it, national minorities are not to determine the state structure, not to modify centralism. "Democratic centralism," as defined in the Party rules, comprises principles which, if applied to the border nationality, are heavily tilted against it. Strict subordination of the minority to the majority and the absolutely binding character of the decisions of higher bodies upon lower bodies doom local independence. In "democratic centralism," centralism is very real and democracy a mere claim. National minorities are not to ask for, nor to be given, constitutional guarantees of a federal character, since these, by their very nature, would affect not only the life of the minority, but also the political and economic structure of the entire state. In a dispute with Polish comrades Lenin stressed that the right to self-determination was not identical with "co-determination." The one presumably was a negative right, the right to leave the state, the other clearly a positive one, the right to participate in the making of the new proletarian multinational state.

"Co-determination" presupposed an agreement between equals, an agreement for the continued existence of the state, though on a proletarian basis. The Great Russian people and a territorial border nationality, however, were not equals either in numbers, or in their cultural level, or in economic or military strength. If "co-determination" was to mean that the small border nationality was to gain real influence upon the making of nation-wide policies, or that it would help to shape the state structure after some federal pattern, it was, according to Lenin, an illusion. "Co-determination" ran counter to the concept of "democratic centralism."

Lenin insisted that "federalism" was "an alliance of equals, an alliance which needs a *general* agreement." [79] Yet he was clearly opposed to a "general" agreement between the Great Russian nationality, that is, its proletariat, and all the other national minorities of Russia. What he considered was a *bilateral* agreement between the Great Russian proletariat and each individual minority. "How can there be a right of one side to the consent of the other side?" he asked Shaumian. [80] Yet there were more than merely two "sides," more than two parties. There were bound to be numerous nationalities in Russia at the time of the "proletarian" revolution, and the Great Russian nationality was, as Lenin himself often stressed, only a minority. [81] How "democratic" was Lenin's refusal, and that of the Bolshevik Party and of the proletariat of the Great Russian people, to deny the likely demand for federalism by so many national minorities— themselves in the aggregate the majority of Russia's population— and to promulgate this policy without prior consultation with them in an ultimatum-like fashion? Democracy and "democratic centralism" were clearly irreconcilable.

While anxious to retain the territorial minorities within Russia, Lenin was unwilling to retain them at the price of federalism. The latter would be economically harmful and an inappropriate political form. The dictatorship of the proletariat necessitated strict centralism and was incompatible with a federal structure.

The conception of federalism played an increasingly important role in Communist theory after the October Revolution.

Yet Lenin had opposed federalism outright and in no uncertain terms[82] in the pre-revolutionary period.

The reversal, radical as it appears, had in some ways been prepared for in the preceding period. In "a few exceptional cases" [83] Lenin had rather early acknowledged the usefulness of the federal principle for the proletarian state, though never for the Party. Later he wrote in a similar vein:

> One may be a decided opponent of this principle [federation], an adherent of democratic centralism, yet one may prefer federalism to legal inequality of nations as the only way to complete democratic centralism.[84]

And he referred in this connection to the "centralist" Marx who had preferred a federation between Ireland and England to the continued oppression of Ireland.

This, however, is hardly a genuine concession to federalism. Federalism is here not preferred to democratic centralism as such; the alternative is only one between federalism and continued oppression of a nationality. Besides, even this conditional concession to federalism is considered a merely temporary one, federalism being "the *only way* to *complete* democratic centralism." [85]

The unitary state in Bolshevik thought was always preferable to the federally organized state. Yet circumstances might well necessitate a choice between two types of state structures, neither of which was unitary. A federal state, while not best suited to the purposes of the fighting proletariat or the victorious working class and Party, might then, temporarily, prove the best solution. And this would certainly be the case when federalism was a mere façade behind which centralism operated. Concessions made to federalism then were merely sham concessions, and respect paid to it merely lip-service, a farce designed to deceive the border nationalities.

CHAPTER FIVE

Nationality Policy After the "Proletarian" Revolution

NATIONAL EQUALITY AND THE PERSISTENCE OF NATIONAL ANTIPATHIES.

Having seized power, the proletariat will have to contend with national hatred, prejudice, and tensions which have been accumulated for generations. National antipathies in the capitalist and imperialist eras had, according to Lenin, been produced by the exploitation of nationalities, but had also sprung from struggles of imperialist nations among themselves. On the other hand, capitalist development speeded up the growth of all means of communication, furthered economic and intellectual exchange, and helped to overcome provincialism and economic and cultural isolation.[1] It laid thus the foundation for closer contacts between states and nationalities, and for cultural assimilation and ethnic amalgamation.[2]

Two countercurrents operated thus under capitalism, one building up new walls of misunderstanding, the other tending to reduce differences between nationalities. The proletariat's, respectively the Party's task after the seizure of power consisted in making ineffective and innocuous the former by eliminating the capitalist foundation and in strengthening the latter.

The "proletarian" revolution will grant equality to all individuals and to all nationalities. It will confer the right to self-determination to all nationalities, though with qualifications; the right to self-determination is the clearest expression of the principle of the equality of nations.

112

The new proletarian state will embrace all those national minorities which have decided against secession. Multinational in character, it is to continue to proclaim and practice equality of nations and to abolish remaining vestiges of national privileges and discrimination.

The "proletarian" dictatorship will, of course, bring about radical economic and social changes, but these alone, important as they are, are not going by themselves to end national oppression. Socialism, "although based on economics . . . is by no means exclusively economics." The abolishment of classes will not automatically bring an end to national oppression.

> By transforming capitalism into socialism, the proletariat creates the *possibility* for the complete abolition of national oppression; this possibility will become *reality* 'only'— 'only'—when complete democracy is introduced in all spheres including the fixing of state boundaries in accordance with the 'sympathies' of the population, and including complete freedom of secession. This in turn will, *in practice,* lead to the complete elimination of all national friction, of all national suspicion.[3]

In addition to social and economic revolution, "socialism" requires "complete democracy." After the "proletarian" revolution democracy must be introduced in all spheres of life. The freedom to secession is a demand of democracy.

At times Lenin insists that the right to self-determination, its mere proclamation, is *the* solution to the nationality question. At other times he seems to suspect that the realization of self-determination will not automatically wipe out the problem of nationality; it will not lead to the disappearance of the multinational state and the formation of numerous nation-states, but, very likely, will bring about the reaffirmation of the polyglot state, though on a new basis. The new proletarian state will, in many cases, be a multinational state. And "national antipathies" [4] are bound to persist for some time after the "proletarian" revolution.

In accordance with its program, the "proletariat," having seized power, will proclaim full equality of all nationalities and abolish discrimination of all sorts, including those based upon national grounds. But it will not be able to abolish capitalism and bourgeois ideology with one stroke. It is also not going to solve the age-old problem of nationality through one or even several decrees. It would, admittedly, be unable to accomplish all this "quickly" under any circumstances. It is the less likely to attain these objectives immediately, since national prejudices, as Lenin seems to contend, exist among the workers of the dominant nationality. The proletariat

> will not have become holy and not be immune merely because it will have effected the social revolution . . . The national antipathies will not quickly vanish . . . from one day to the next. The hate—and indeed quite justified hate—of the oppressed nationalities will *still exist* for some time; it will vanish only *after* the victory of socialism and *after* the full establishment of completely democratic relations between the nations.[5]

National antipathies will continue to persist after the "proletarian" revolution, throughout the period of the dictatorship of the proletariat. Their disappearance will depend not only on the "victory of socialism" internally, but also on the "full establishment of completely democratic relations" between the nationalities. Not only the "victory of socialism," but also a "victory of democracy" is required to bring about a solution of the nationality question.

After the "proletarian" revolution the Party had to continue to work toward the elimination of national hatred and antipathies by means of a truly international education, to proclaim and practice national self-determination, and to uphold national equality. Such a policy was bound to reduce national tensions. Lenin also expressed the hope and belief that the natural process of assimilation of nationalities, operative under capitalism, would continue under the proletarian state and under socialism, and contribute toward national peace.

ASSIMILATION. COSMOPOLITANISM OR INTERNATIONALISM?

For the stages prior to the "proletarian" revolution Lenin had, as already pointed out, favored national assimilation and had been opposed especially to the development of the culture of backward and primitive nationalities.[6] It was his view that it was not the task of the proletariat and of the Bolshevik Party to develop the national culture of "every nation."[7] Lenin stressed the importance in the bourgeois-capitalist period of joint proletarian political, economic, and cultural organizations, linking the workers of all nationalities in the struggle against the ruling classes. He emphasized the significance of "unity" among the various proletarian organizations of different ethnic background and the desirability of their "amalgamation."[8] The merger of proletarian organizations would lessen national differences and further the assimilation of nationalities.[9]

Joint organizations of all the workers of Russia, whatever their individual nationality, were not only essential if the party was to be an effective fighting instrument of the proletariat, but also important from the viewpoint of combatting nationalism under bourgeois capitalism *and* after the "proletarian" revolution.

Beyond the "unity" of the workers of different nationalities and their organizational "amalgamation," extensively propagated by Lenin, lay hidden a more ambitious objective, namely the broader and more far-reaching goal of amalgamation and assimilation of entire nationalities. Assimilation of nationalities is only rejected, if attempted by "application of national force, oppression and legal inequality."

The proletariat supports everything which contributes to the elimination of national differences, to tearing down the barriers between nations, everything which makes the relations of the nationalities to each other increasingly more intimate, everything which leads to the *amalgamation of nations*. . . . Marxism replaces . . . nationalism with internationalism, with the amalgamation of all nationalities in a higher unity. . . . Economics will amalgamate the different nationalities.[10]

"Assimilation," "amalgamation" (sliianie), a "higher unity" than nationality—all this points to the future extinction of nationalities, to cosmopolitanism rather than to internationalism.[11]

In a letter to Shaumian, Lenin, while criticizing the latter's view "that Bolshevism should come out for a single state language," rejects any law or force necessary to institute it; he does not question, however, "the indisputably *progressive significance* of centralization, of large states, of the *single language*."[12] Uniformity rather than diversity is the keynote. And uniformity appears as a guarantee of unity.

Lenin commits himself and the Party to more—and in some respects to less—than internationalism. True internationalism, based upon the acknowledgment of existing nationalities, is dedicated to spreading international understanding. It sees the nationalities realistically with all their virtues and their weaknesses. Its clear purpose is to remove obstacles to the cooperation and peaceful living together of the nations of the world. It is based upon the conviction that the mere difference of national character and outlook does not create animosity. It attacks the causes of war, economic, social, political, and psychological ones. But it rests its case upon the basically optimistic foundation that unity can be safely anchored upon cultural and linguistic diversity and does not require uniformity either of form or content.

Lenin, however, as if doubts would plague him as to the feasibility of basing unity upon diversity, inclines to a degree plainly inconsistent with the professed Marxist world view toward uniformity, a uniformity not only of content, but also of form.[13] Proletarian, socialist, international culture, instead of bourgeois, capitalist, and national culture, is not enough. Assimilation of nationalities will lead to their "amalgamation," to "a higher unity" than that of nationality.[14]

The "higher unity" will be an ethnical as well as a political unity. It will be based upon a "single language," but will point also toward a wide, all-embracing political unit.

> Just as mankind can achieve abolition of classes only by passing through the transition period of the dictatorship of the oppressed class, so mankind can achieve the inevitable *merging of nations* only by passing through the transition period of complete liberation of all the oppressed nations, i.e. their freedom to secede.[15]

The right to secession thus forms the link, the necessary intermediate stage, between the capitalist multinational state and the ultimate "inevitable merging of nations" under proletarian aegis. "The aim of socialism," Lenin holds, is not only to abolish the "present division of mankind into small states" and

> all-national isolation, not only to bring nations closer to each other, but also to merge them.[16]

The introduction of "complete democracy," "including complete freedom of secession," he holds in another connection, will result in

> the speedy establishment of intimacy between and amalgamation of nations, culminating in the 'withering away' of the state.[17]

The "merger" is thought by Lenin to have ethnic and political significance. The Party was not only opposed to "economic disintegration" and "in favor of large states," but also favored "closer unity," "even" "fusion of nations." [18] The possible previous secession of the border nationality had likewise political and ethnic aspects. The formation of an independent political entity by the seceding nationality was bound to deepen its national consciousness.

If political and ethnic "amalgamation" of nationalities was the unavoidable, and at the same time desirable goal, historical development certainly took remarkable detours by turning first toward political and ethnic separation, and then in the opposite direction toward political and ethnic "amalgamation." Yet Lenin apparently held this "course" to be in accordance with Marxian dialectics.

That Lenin favored assimilation was no doubt an inconsistency from the viewpoint of Marxism. Marxism maintained that dissension and strife between various nations and nationalities grew out of capitalism and imperialism. The overthrow of the capitalist order by the proletariat would establish peaceable relations among the different nationalities. Marxism likewise asserted that discord and conflict among nations and natural national differences, such as consisted in national character, in habits, in customs, and in outlook, were by no means causally linked. Disputes among nations were rooted only in the economic order of capitalism and in imperialism, its offshoot. They were not the mere outgrowth of natural differences, such as the national character.

Marxists, therefore, ought to be emotionally unaffected by the multiplicity and variety of nationalities and national characters in the world and be neither depressed by their increase nor elated by their decline. Whether there are two nationalities or two hundred ought to make little difference in regard to the likelihood of peace on earth, provided national strife is, as Marxism claims, rooted exclusively in certain types of the economic and social structure. Lenin's delight over the natural process of assimilation, operative, according to him, in the stages before and after the "proletarian" revolution, is therefore incomprehensible.

CHAPTER SIX

Conclusion

The right to self-determination is to Lenin the magic key which opens all doors to the problem of nationality. It is the center toward which all proletarian thought and action gravitates, or ought to gravitate. It is not only the means to the end, but, he claims, also the end itself; not merely the slogan apt to rally during the bourgeois-capitalist stage the proletariat and other social strata of the oppressed nationalities to the colors of the Great Russian proletariat, but also the solution of the nationality problem under the proletarian state and under socialism.

The slogan of the right to national self-determination is, according to Lenin, a tactical imperative. It assures the Great Russian proletariat or the proletariat of any other dominant nationality the sympathy and active help of the oppressed nationalities prior to and during the "proletarian" revolution. This slogan is therefore clearly in the interests of the proletariat and of socialism.

The right to national self-determination is also a "democratic" demand. It is one of the demands of political democracy, advanced by the liberal bourgeoisie. While, in general, the proletariat will uphold all demands of political democracy, including national self-determination, the interests of the proletariat and of socialism and the interests of bourgeois political democracy do not always coincide. Where a conflict of a tactical nature arises between them, political democracy must always be subordinated to proletarian and socialist interests. This also holds true of national self-determination. The primacy of socialism is thus never in doubt.

Acknowledging the primacy of socialism, however, does not justify overlooking the revolutionary potentiality of the nationality problem. Yet the Party's left wing on the nationality question is, according to Lenin, guilty of ignoring the reality of national oppression and also of political and tactical shortsightedness. It disregards the tremendous importance of the national movement as a potential ally of the fighting proletariat. The left wing, unwilling to make any concessions to the national liberation movement, promises the solution of all problems, including the national one, by the "proletarian" revolution and, ultimately, by socialism and communism. It appeals to the oppressed nationalities to be patient and to have faith in the saving power of socialism.

Lenin holds that this approach, based upon " 'postponing' " [1] the satisfaction of the justified national desires of oppressed nationalities, is bound to be tactically harmful. It is neither going to strengthen the Party, nor to gain allies for the proletariat. To the contrary, it is likely to drive a wedge between the proletariat and the oppressed nationalities. In Lenin's view, the internationalist wing of the Party is pursuing indefensible tactics on the nationality question and, thus, instead of accelerating the "proletarian" revolution, will delay its oncoming.

Tactical considerations make Lenin criticize the Party's left wing on the nationality question, though he praises its international outlook and motivation. Ideological considerations, on the other hand, the belief in the primacy of socialism at all times under all circumstances, make him excoriate the Party's right wing, the "socialist" proponents of "national-cultural autonomy." The left wing's sin is of a tactical nature, the right wing's is a crime of an ideological character; the first is politically shortsighted, the latter betrays doctrine, it is heretical. The right wing leans toward nationalism and, in Lenin's view, makes dangerously large concessions to it.

The slogan of the right to national self-determination, if unqualified, represents itself a significant concession of the proletariat and of the Party to nationalism. It constitutes an encouragement of the national movement. From the viewpoint of proletarian and socialist interests this concession can only be tactically justified. Upholding the right to national self-determination will, according to Lenin, not only gain allies for the proletariat among oppressed nationalities, but will also create unity within the Party and will help to fight nationalism and national strife.

Lenin combats nationalism in every respect. Struggle against it is one of his main concerns. And he holds the right to national self-determination not to be an encouragement of nationalism, but rather a weapon to fight it.[2]

While the ruling classes of the oppressor and of the oppressed nationalities gather under the banner of nationalism and wage their battles under its sign, the proletariat must meet them on their own ground, oppose their national program with a national program of its own; it must raise the flag of national self-determination.

The right wing, however, according to Lenin, does not fight nationalism, it has surrendered to it. Against the Right's concept of national culture, a weapon also of the bourgeoisie, Lenin raises the idea of international culture. He excoriates the socialist proponents of "national-cultural autonomy," a concept which, he fears, tends to split the unitary Party along national lines. He also opposes national-cultural autonomy because it "guarantees," perpetuates, and also develops the culture of all nationalities, those scattered throughout the state and already on the road to assimilation, and those which nationally have not yet awakened. The concept of national-cultural autonomy, besides threatening to blunt the fighting weapon of the proletariat and the Party, stands also in the way of the assimilation of nationalities.

Lenin, however, hails assimilation of nationalities as "progressive" in all stages and as contributing, as he claims, to the speedy approach of the "proletarian" revolution. He pleads for unity and amalgamation of the proletarian organizations of the diverse nationalities, from the viewpoint again of proletarian and socialist interests. Not cultural and national diversity, but rather assimilation is his goal. Nationalism within the ranks of the Party, within its organization as well as in the proletarian state, is not encouraged, but plainly and unmistakably opposed.

Why does Lenin boost nationalism by means of the slogan of self-determination to oppose it bitterly at other times? He opposes consistently the concepts of national culture and of national-cultural autonomy on account of their bourgeois class character. He supports, however, the program of national self-determination, because he considers it, on the whole, to be in the interest of the proletarian class struggle and of socialism. In case the slogan should at any time clash with the interests of the proletariat and of socialism, it must, Lenin insists, yield to these higher interests. The numerous qualifications to self-determination which he establishes are designed to guarantee their supremacy.

Having given through the adoption of the slogan of national self-determination—a tactical imperative—an unavoidable stimulus to nationalism, Lenin, on second thought, appears to have become alarmed by the magnitude of the concession made, and, in a hurry, tries to erect safeguards to dam the powerful current of nationalism. He establishes so many exceptions to the right to national self-determination that little, if anything, remains of this concept. He may have held that his numerous theoretical qualifications to the right of national self-determination would not appreciably diminish the propagandistic value of the slogan, while having a powerful restraining effect upon the Party and the proletariat of the oppressed nationality prior to, during, and after the "proletarian" revolution.

The numerous qualifications should have made the national minorities wary and suspicious of Lenin's and the Bolsheviks' nationality program. Yet, in the heat of the struggle, face to face with many political groups and parties which were either outright hostile to self-determination and autonomy or evasive, pleading *general* democratic reform, many among the national minorities prior to 1917 fastened their hopes upon the glittering promises which Lenin's and the Bolsheviks' nationality program seemed to offer, without subjecting it to a critical and searching analysis.

Self-determination, Lenin holds, will become general during the "proletarian" revolution. The victorious proletariat must grant the oppressed nationalities the right to self-determination at the earliest possible moment.

National self-determination will then lead either to a separate political status or to the reaffirmation of the multinational state, though on the new basis of full national equality. The nationality which has seceded will retain the sovereign right of reconsideration, in accordance with national self-determination. The nationality, however, which has cast its lot with the multinational state, has, an analysis of Lenin's respective views reveals, thus relinquished any further right to national self-determination.

During the stages of proletarian dictatorship and of socialism and communism, the right to national self-determination will therefore be exercised only by a minority of nationalities, that minority which during the bourgeois-capitalist era and during the "proletarian" revolution has seceded, but later wishes to return to the proletarian or socialist multinational realm.

While Lenin recognizes the right of the nationality to self-determination before and immediately after the "proletarian" seizure of power, he stresses the economic advantages of the large state in all phases, even under capitalism; the large state, of course, is the multinational state. It is clearly in the interests of the proletariat, of socialism, and of internationalism, and, other conditions being equal, preferable to the small one. While the proletariat of the oppressor nation must grant the oppressed nationalities the right to a state of their own, to secession, the proletariat of the oppressed nationality has, according to Lenin, the socialist duty to insist upon the "right to union."

The slogan of national self-determination is of vital importance in all stages prior to the "proletarian" revolution and especially at the time of the seizure of power, during the "proletarian" revolution. However, the tactical usefulness of the slogan of national self-determination comes largely to an end with the establishment of the "proletarian" dictatorship.

Lenin was well aware of the merely temporary value of the slogan. Though upholding the right to self-determination, he considered secession of a nationality after the "proletarian" seizure of power as a reactionary step, economically harmful, culturally merely delaying a beneficial assimilation, and unnecessary in view of the newly established national equality in the polyglot state. Yet could he, before 1917, possibly reveal that national self-determination had only tactical significance without undermining his nationality policy and the national program of the Bolshevik Party? Lenin became thus the prisoner of his own slogan. This slogan, needed prior to the "proletarian" revolution, could not be disavowed for the stages following the "proletarian" seizure of power.[3] This would have abruptly ended its usefulness. A shrewd tactician, Lenin rather hid his real convictions and insisted upon the right to national self-determination in all stages, not only prior to and during, but also after the "proletarian" revolution.

Yet Lenin could not always and completely conceal his true convictions. And at times they stand out rather sharply and appear irreconcilable with genuine national self-determination. At other times his silence betrays him.

The right to self-determination, Lenin insists, is not equivalent to actual secession. To plead for self-determination does not necessarily mean encouraging the formation of small states. While he does not wish a multinational state which is based upon compulsion, but one based on a "free union," he leaves little doubt that he wishes a "union."

Since the right to national self-determination is arbitrarily and narrowly conceived as the right to secession, the many nationalities in the interior are deprived of all national rights. Neither they nor the border nationalities may demand any concessions in the nature of federalism or autonomy. The proletariat and the Party do not recognize any "right" on their part to either federalism or autonomy; they will always reject the former, but will graciously consent to the latter. Any negotiations concerning possible guarantees between the border nationalities and the formerly dominant nationality—as might befit equals—is thus precluded. The much vaunted equality of nations which is to begin with the "proletarian" revolution dissipates into thin air. Not only can the border nationality not raise any demands and pose any conditions prior to joining the multinational state, but its "self-determination" is reduced to a single decision, the decision on whether to leave the multinational state or to remain within it. If it has made the latter decision, it has no further rights at all. It has ceased to forge its own fate, which hence will be entirely in the hands of the multinational state.

Last but not least: Who in the stages of the "proletarian" revolution and proletarian dictatorship is, according to Lenin, to exercise the right to self-determination? Who is to vote in the regional "referendum"? Does the fate of the border region lie in the hands of the entire border nationality, or is it merely the regional proletariat which is to make the final decision? A proletariat forming the majority or a minority of the border nationality? What is the relation of the border proletariat to the Party? Would the latter accept an adverse decision of the border proletariat?

Most of these crucial questions are not even raised by Lenin. His failure to do so arouses doubts as to the genuineness of his concept of self-determination. Secession in the stages of the proletarian revolution, proletarian dictatorship, and thereafter, was probably held so unlikely as not to warrant a detailed discussion. Another possible interpretation is that Lenin did not wish to elaborate upon these problems, all closely linked with secession, because he was resolved not to permit it. He did not pose the foregoing questions in order to spare himself future embarrassment.

Yet in the summer of 1913 the Party had gone on record that each case of national self-determination was to be decided separately, to be judged on its own merits, i.e. on its effect upon general "democratic" and proletarian-socialist interests.[4] The Party then felt it imperative to assert its supremacy, its right to a veto, in the matter of national self-determination, in view of the considerable national stirrings and the growing strength of the national movement inside and outside Party ranks. It may have counted on the circumstance that its contradictions and inconsistencies on the nationality question would still elude the masses of oppressed nationalities, while its propaganda on nationality would retain in their eyes its lustre of sincerity and justice, and thus its effectiveness.

Lenin's thought on the nationality question, conceived and developed with an eye on the "proletarian" seizure of power, is designed to facilitate it and to ensure the success of the "proletarian" revolution. It has thus a logic of its own. Yet judged from any other viewpoint than that of tactical need, and that includes also that of Marxism, there are a large number of sharp contradictions and basic incongruities in Lenin's thought on nationality, to say nothing of wide gaps.

An all-pervading dichotomy characterizes Lenin's thought on nationality. On the one hand, there is his pure negativism in regard to nationality and the national state—based upon his conviction of the transient character of nationalism—his approval of assimilation and cosmopolitanism, instead of national culture and nationalism. On the other hand, there is his insistence, in spite of all qualifications, on national self-determination.

It is Lenin's conviction that this slogan is a tactical necessity which alone makes him accept it and advance it persistently in spite of all his natural inclinations to the contrary.

Numerous incongruities in Lenin's thought on nationality spring from the foregoing dichotomy. These contradictions reflect his ambivalence in regard to nationality and nationalism. He rejects nationalism as a goal and tolerates it only as an unavoidable, transitory stage of social development. The internationalist in Lenin does not and cannot hide his aversion to it; the tactician in him, however, endorses nationalism in the form of national liberation, though only conditionally. After having approved it, he turns then to the herculean task of making nationality palatable to a Party which, dedicated to internationalism, has always opposed nationalism in any form.

The slogan of the right to national self-determination, by encouraging nationalism, national culture, and the smaller state, might, Lenin realizes, operate against the interests of the proletariat and of socialism. The long-range proletarian and socialist interests, even the short-term ones, demand international culture, amalgamation of nations and nationalities, a large, meaning a multi-national state. Yet the tactical advantages of Lenin's nationality program more than balanced, in his mind, any possible harm the slogan might temporarily cause. By holding out the promise of self-determination, the proletariat of the dominant nationality would win friends and allies among the working class and other social groups of the oppressed nationalities.

Tactical considerations, it could be argued, made Lenin even adopt positions which clearly ran counter to Marxism. His joy, for instance, over assimilation and his favoring "amalgamation"—hardly reconcilable with his insistence on upholding the right to national self-determination and on encouraging, within limits, national impulses—was, by implication, an abandonment of Marxist tenets.[5] Marxism demanded internationalism, but not cosmopolitanism, not the disappearance and the extinction of nationalities. Marxism saw the root of national hate, of national tensions, and of imperialism in economics and in the class struggle, but not in nationality as such. It was not Marxism which made Lenin rejoice over ethnic assimilation. His realistic perception of the strength of national feelings and national movements, his persuasion, especially after 1913, of the powerful hold of nationalism upon the proletariat made him fear nationalism as a rival of socialism among the national groups; therefore his elation over the assimilation, the extinction of some nationalities, the removal of some obstacles on the road to socialism.

Lenin tried his best to turn into an asset what appeared at first glance a liability to the socialist proletariat and the Party. Nationalism was not to be a competitor, but an ally of the proletariat and of socialism. A brilliant tactician, he conceived early the significance of the slogan of the right to national self-determination as a bridge linking the revolutionary proletariat of the dominant nation with the oppressed nationalities in an alliance which could be vitally important for both. That the national movement, potentially hostile to socialism, could be made to serve the latter's purposes seemed to Lenin to be in accordance with the demands of revolutionary tactics as well as in conformity with the intricacies of materialist dialectics.

CHAPTER SEVEN

Lenin and Communist Theory and Practice of Self-Determination After the February Revolution

The February Revolution unleashed tremendous new forces throughout Russia. It also gave strong impulses to the national movements of the numerous non-Russian nationalities and made some of them raise the demand for national independence.

The Bolsheviks entered the political arena in 1917 armed with Lenin's nationality program, though still only few among them displayed genuine enthusiasm for it. Yet the resolution on the national question adopted at the Seventh Conference of the RSDRP in April, 1917—the first detailed statement of the Party's nationality policy after the February Revolution— was in its entirety a reaffirmation of Lenin's already well known principles of nationality policy, including the recognition of the right of all nationalities "which belong to Russia to free separation and formation of an independent state." But at the same time it was stressed, as it already had been in the Party Resolution of the summer of 1913, that the question of the desirability of separation "of this or that nation at this or that moment" had to be determined "in each case" separately, "namely from the viewpoint of the interests of the entire social development and of the proletarian class struggle for socialism."[1] National self-determination was thus sharply circumscribed; the Party, leaving all doors open, could decide on practically any course, on approving secession in one and refusing it in another case. This position, of course, was fully in accord with Lenin's previously expressed opportunistic views on the matter.

129

The right to national self-determination continued to be propagated throughout the year 1917. In June, the First Congress of Soviets, in which the Social Revolutionaries controlled a majority and the Bolsheviks had only a small minority, proclaimed the right to self-determination,[2] though with qualifications, and in October the Second Congress of Soviets confirmed this stand.[3]

The October Revolution of 1917 was basically a Great Russian Revolution. It was supported by groups and individuals belonging to all of Russia's nationalities though it was also opposed by people of diverse ethnic backgrounds. The acknowledged leadership of the proletariat over the peasantry, under the then existing conditions of the Great Russian and the other nationalities, meant hegemony of the Great Russian working class over the peasants of the different nationalities of Russia. This was also reflected in the ethnic composition of the Communist Party in this period. In 1922, 71.96% of the members of the Party were Great Russians, though their percentage of the total population was only 52.91%.[4] And Mikhail Kalinin blurted out the truth when he said that the aim of the Soviet government was to " 'teach the people of the Khirgiz steppe, the small Uzbek cotton-grower, and the Turkmenian gardener to accept the ideals of the Leningrad worker'."[5]

Yet such voices were drowned since October, 1917, by the numerous and high-sounding pronunciamentos assuring the non-Russian nationalities the end of all discriminatory policies and individual and national freedom and equality. Immediately after the October Revolution, on November 2, 1917, the Council of People's Commissars issued a declaration of the rights of the nationalities of Russia, signed by Lenin as chairman and by Stalin as Commissar for Nationalities, reasserting the equality and "sovereignty" of the nationalities of Russia and their right to free self-determination, "which may include the separation and formation of an independent state."[6] After the seizure of power the newly established communist government did not repudiate its nationality program, neither directly nor by remaining silent; to the contrary, in the first hours of victory it reasserted it strongly and loudly.

The Bolsheviks had proclaimed the right to self-determination so long that a repudiation was hardly feasible. Also, having taken over a militarily vanquished state, they could not count on preventing the secession of those nationalities which were in control of the border regions and ardently desired separation. Under these circumstances, Lenin's nationality policy, by "permitting" secession and creating the impression of Bolshevik honesty and generosity, could, as Lenin had always insisted, have only beneficial integrating effects; such a policy was bound to create confidence and to tie hesitating nationalities more closely to the Bolshevik-dominated Great Russian core.

Bolshevism was then not merely aiming at preserving as much as possible of the Tsarist patrimony. It looked upon the Russian revolution as the beginning of a revolution which was to encompass Europe, Asia, and the entire world. It early made clear that the slogan of the right to national self-determination had not only national, but international significance, that it expected its nationality program to serve not only as a rallying point for the formerly oppressed nationalities of Russia, but also to prove a means to lure additional adjoining nationalities to the Soviet realm. In a special appeal "To all Muslim Toilers of Russia and the East," which played as much upon recent religious as upon national oppression, Moslem "workers" were assured of the "new right" of organizing their national life "in complete freedom," and even Moslems who had formerly not been subjects of Russia were promised aid in overthrowing their oppressors.[7]

But soon the principle of self-determination was substantially qualified. In December, 1917, and January, 1918, Stalin, Commissar of Nationalities, "granted" it "to the toilers," but refused it to the bourgeoisie."[8] Novel and far-reaching as this official interpretation was, it was implied in earlier policy statements drafted by Lenin himself—reserving the decision as to the policy on self-determination "in each case" to the Party—and anticipated in an early interpretation of this concept—which stands rather by itself—as a right only of the working class of the nationalities concerned.[9] Yet in all his other writings on the nationality question Lenin had refrained from limiting the right to self-determination specifically to the proletariat.

The Eighth Party Congress, held in March, 1919—in the same month in which the Communist International was founded —adopted a new Party program. It reasserted the right to national self-determination and defined it again as the "right to political secession." Its recognition was necessary "to overcome the suspicion of the toiling masses of the oppressed countries" [10] against the proletariat of the formerly dominant states—hardly a positive ground for establishing a new national state. The resolution did not pose the question as to who was the carrier of the nation's will; yet granting or refusing support for the secession of a particular nationality was left to the determination by the Party, which was to "take into consideration the stage of historical development of the given nation." This position differed little from the earlier Resolutions on the nationality question, adopted prior to the February Revolution and thereafter.

Lenin's characteristic formulation of nationality policy, namely "proletarian" support for the principle of self-determination coupled with the Party's opposition to it in a particular case, emerges also in these policy statements of the years 1917, 1918, and 1919. The underlying thought as well as the phraseology in them are clearly Lenin's.

After the February Revolution, the Bolsheviks had, in accordance with their nationality policy, supported the national minority movements, mainly to embarrass the Provisional Government. But after their seizure of power in October, 1917, they, in order to preserve their territorial legacy, suppressed many national, centrifugal tendencies, while continuing to pay

lip-service to the right to national self-determination, to secession. Their dilemma became acute after the peace of Brest
Litovsk in March, 1918, when they were forced by the victorious German armies to cede vast and rich territories inhabited largely by non-Great Russian nationalities. Germany's
military defeat, imposed upon the country by the Western
powers later in the year, opened up new possibilities for Soviet
Russia, then torn by the Civil War, to retrieve grievous losses.
In the ensuing dispute between the demands of practical politics
and those of theory, the former gained a quick and decisive
triumph; the theory had always been shot through with incongruities and outright contradictions.[11]

After the October Revolution Soviet governments were
set up in the Baltic states, in Latvia, and Estonia. Subsequently
dissolved by German troops, these Soviet republics were re-
stored after Germany's defeat by Soviet Russian armies which
also established a republic in Lithuania. These Baltic republics
were finally overwhelmed by anti-Bolshevik national troops
supported by the Allies.[12]

Soviet troops intervened also in January, 1918, in Finland
to assist Finnish and Red Guards in the attempt to establish
a Soviet government, though the Bolsheviks had recognized the
independence of the country only in December, 1917. In 1920,
Soviet Russia again recognized the sovereignty and independence
of all these states.

Superior military force, not Bolshevik recognition of democracy and of national self-determination, had determined the
outcome of these struggles.

This also holds true of the fighting in the Ukraine and
in White Russia, the outcome of which was favorable for the
Soviets. In the Ukraine, after a desperate, many-cornered and
often confused struggle, during which Russian Soviet troops
intervened on the side of the Ukrainian Soviets against the
broadly representative Ukrainian Rada, the Russian Red Army
established definite control in the summer of 1921. A White

Russian Soviet Socialist Republic had already been proclaimed by the invading Soviet troops on January 1st, 1919. Likewise, repeated intervention by Soviet armies in Armenia, Azerbaidjan, and Georgia in the years 1920 and 1921 decided the fate of the Transcaucasian Republics.

The emerging pattern was unmistakable: In the life-and-death struggle of the Civil War, principles counted for little, and regaining vital border regions, which were the seats of important industries and the sources for Russia's food and fuel, was prized greatly. During this war the Communist Party had made political capital with its slogan of national self-determination, though it violated it in practice repeatedly.

When the guns were silenced, Soviet Russia counted her gains and losses. Many border nationalities had established their new independent states; over others, Great Russian Bolshevism, assisted by native Bolsheviks, had asserted its control. Yet the nationalism of the latter nationalities had not completely lost the battle. It had wrung from Bolshevism important concessions in the form of the national-territorial structure of the state and of linguistic-cultural autonomy. Politically suppressed, nationalism reasserted itself with new vigor in 1922, in the period of the consolidation of the Soviet state.

The urgency of the nationality problem was also reflected in bitter intra-Party disputes at this time. A Party crisis in Georgia in the fall of 1922 over the federation of Transcaucasia and its manner and tempo, resulted in the resignation of the entire Georgian Central Committee, and brought the nationality question anew to the attention of Lenin. He was seriously ill at that time.

Lenin immediately perceived the far-reaching significance of the conflict over Georgia,[13] its importance not only for the Party but also for the future of Russia. Privately he blamed the extreme Great Russian nationalism of communist officials for the rift, and promptly "declared war on Great Russian chauvinism." [14] At the same time he hastened to appoint an investigating commission which was headed by Dzerzhinskii and consisted entirely of persons of non-Russian origin, a group which could be expected to be impartial in a dispute involving Georgian and Great Russian communists. The report of the commission, however, exonerated Stalin and Ordzonikidze who had conceived and executed the policies leading to the Georgian crisis. Lenin, extremely critical of the commission's report,[15] insisted that Comrade Ordzonikidze should be "exemplarily punished" and "that Stalin and Dzerzhinskii must be held politically responsible for this truly Great Russian nationalistic campaign." [16]

Lenin was preparing a "bombshell for Stalin" [17] at the Twelfth Party Congress when he suffered his third stroke. The illness which silenced Lenin played into Stalin's hands. But there can be no doubt about the existence of a sharp disagreement between both men during the last year of Lenin's life. And one of the major areas of dissension was the nationality question.

In spite of their serious rift[18] on the occasion of the Party crisis in Georgia in 1922, Lenin and Stalin held similar views on the nationality problem and policy. They agreed in principle on the nationalities' right to secession, on the need of qualifying and even nullifying it in a particular case, and on the subordination of national desires to the interests of the proletariat and of socialism. But in their methods, their tone, the consideration shown to formerly oppressed nationalities, there was a distinct difference between them, a difference which to a large degree was rooted in their personalities. Yet there were also differences other than those of approach and personality, which are only concealed by Stalin's apparent endorsement of the ultimate goal of cosmopolitanism. They disagreed in regard to the fostering and development of national languages and national cultures and in regard to the question of the desirability of assimilation of nationalities.[19]

Some differences in Lenin's and Stalin's views on the nationality question were already noticeable as early as 1913, when
Stalin, under Lenin's guidance, had written his essay "Marxism
and the National Question." [20] They became more pronounced
after the February Revolution, when the "assimilated non-
Russian" [21] Stalin adopted a more nationalistic, Great Russian
line,[22] while Lenin, though in general approving the centralistic
course and not hesitating to violate self-determination, if necessary, repeatedly warned that tact and understanding were required in dealing with formerly oppressed nationalities; he was
fearful that a chauvinist course would repel the downtrodden
and dependent nationalities and rob communist propaganda
of its trump cards. Yet in the matter of fostering national
languages and cultures Stalin was the more "liberal" one.

It was in connection with the Georgian Party crisis that
Lenin wrote several letters late in 1922; though they were not
made public at the time, their content became partly known.
These letters, a most valuable source, reveal his uneasiness in
the matter of Soviet nationality policy. He voices therein no
doubt about the theoretical correctness of Bolshevik nationality
policy, but rather holds that actual Soviet policy has swerved
from the correct course. It is not that one or the other feature
of the Party's nationality doctrine and program has proven
wrong; it is rather that the executors of Soviet nationality policy
have failed.

What are the reasons offered for the failure of the communist nationality policy? Lenin blames the bureaucracy and
the bureaucrats, but also points to the lack of a truly communist
doctrine. He castigates the "Russian apparatus which . . .
was borrowed from Tsarism and only barely anointed with
the Soviet chrism," [23] an apparatus "still thoroughly alien to us,"
"representing a bourgeois Tsarist mechanism which we had no
opportunity of conquering";[24] the typical Russian bureaucrat is
branded a "scoundrel and violator." [25] Yet the most prominent
men involved in the dispute were Stalin, Dzerzhinskii, and

Ordzonikidze, clearly none of them either "bourgeois" or "tsarist."

Lenin traces the failure of Bolshevik nationality policy also to failings of communists in other respects than merely those of doctrine. He blames also the misbehavior of Bolsheviks, their "irritability" and "endless coercions of and insults" [26] against the minorities. Nothing is more dangerous to the development and consolidation of proletarian class solidarity than "national injustice." What is required is not mere "formal equality," but a real one. "A truly proletarian attitude requires of us extraordinary caution, courtesy and complaisance." The difficulties in Georgia arose, it becomes clear, because leading communists, instead of adopting such a "proletarian attitude," had displayed a wrong one and had clung to the "petty bourgeois viewpoint." Yet for the proletariat it is "not only important but essentially indispensable to win for itself the maximum of confidence in the proletarian class struggle." It is "better to stretch too far in the direction of complaisance and softness toward the national minorities than too little." [27]

Doubts have arisen in Lenin. "The 'freedom of exit from the Union,' with which we justify ourselves," he wrote, will prove to be "nothing but a scrap of paper, incapable of defending the minorities in Russia from the inroads of . . . the Great Russian chauvinist," [28] meaning the Great Russian nationalist communist official. There was no comparable passage in Lenin's writings on the nationality question prior to the February Revolution. Never before had Lenin talked or written of the program of self-determination as a mere "scrap of paper." He always had maintained that the mere propagation of the slogan of the right to national self-determination would solve the nationality problem in Russia and elsewhere. Now, after the "proletarian" seizure of power, he had come to realize the magnitude of a problem of which he had been only dimly aware of before; it was an administrative and at the same time a human problem. Having been inclined to underestimate the problem of administration under the proletarian dictatorship and under socialism,[29] he has now begun to perceive the importance not only of charting a correct policy, but also of carrying it out.

Lenin has now gained a conception of the difficulties of executing what he considered a Bolshevik and just nationality policy by means of the imperfect human instrument he possessed, the Great Russian communist; the latter exhibited "bourgeois" and "chauvinist" tendencies. There were now some doubts in Lenin which had never plagued him before. And he was the more concerned since he realized the importance of the issues at stake. The future of the Soviet state, of the expansion of communism and of the Soviet Union, was in question.

> It would be unforgivable if, on the eve of the emergence of the East and at the beginning of its awakening, we should undermine our prestige there with even the slightest rudeness or injustice to our own minorities.[30]

There was danger that we "ourselves fall into something like imperialistic relations toward the oppressed nationalities."

The foregoing analysis contained the remedy. It lay, according to Lenin, in the adoption of a new, "truly proletarian attitude," in a sort of "indemnification, in one way or another, by means of behavior or concessions in regard to the minorities," [31] in the adoption of new "codes of behavior" for communist officials, in stretching rather "too far" in the "direction of complaisance and softness toward the national minorities" than "too little."

This view was not the one which came to prevail in the Party in the field of nationality policy, not even while Lenin was alive. The Twelfth Congress of the Communist Party, which opened in Moscow in April, 1923, rejected all suggestions which the ailing Lenin had made. It voiced its opposition to curtailing the centralization of the state. It acquitted Stalin and Ordzonikidze. It also rejected Lenin's recommendation of leaning over backwards toward the formerly oppressed nationalities and refused any sort of "indemnification"; it applauded Stalin when he, in pointed reference to Lenin and his criticism of himself, warned that it was not advisable to "stretch too far" in any direction.

The Party seemed in no mood to apologize to the national minorities, either for past oppression under Tsarism nor for any possible mistakes made more recently, since the "proletarian" seizure of power.

There was then clearly noticeable in Lenin's letters a tone of sincerity and genuine regret over the exhibitions of Great Russian chauvinism under communist guise. Yet it should be recalled that Lenin after the October Revolution had often been directly responsible for the actual violation of the principle of self-determination. Also, his apparent sincerity in these letters would have been more convincing, if he had not given so clear expression to his fear of an adverse impact of the possible failure of Soviet nationality policy upon the Soviet Union and communism at large. Basically, it was not on grounds of morality or theoretical consistency, but on account of tactical considerations, that Lenin regretted the nationalist excesses of some of his comrades in the border provinces. Even in these letters of 1922, his last significant utterances, his political testament on the nationality question, Lenin's essentially tactical approach to the nationality question, always paramount with him, reveals itself unmistakably.

Notes

NOTES FOR INTRODUCTION

1. This was *Who are the Friends of the People?* See *Sochineniia,* Second Ed., 30 vols. (Moscow, 1926-32), I.

2. E. H. Carr, *The Bolshevik Revolution 1917-23* (N. Y., 1951), I, 418.

3. While Lenin's "attitude" on the national question was "already defined at the beginning of 1903" (*Ibid.,* 420), his ideas on nationality and national policy were not yet fully developed in this early period. But there is no reason to question that Lenin's ideas during 1913 and thereafter "were the logical development of the position on the national question he held in the period of the Second Congress" in 1903 (See Editors' Notes, Lenin, *Soch.,* XVII, 421). It was only Lenin's views on *Party* organization, and with it on national-cultural autonomy, which were fully developed and well established in the decade prior to 1913; they, admittedly, foreshadowed Lenin's and the Bolsheviks' position on the national question also on the *state* level.

In 1913 Lenin began to display unusual interest in the nationality question. In the summer he presented his views on the national problem at several occasions, at a meeting of Party members in Poronin, Galicia, at a students' gathering at the University of Krakau, and in Bern (*Soch.,* XVII, 91); in his own words, he had then studied "a little" the nationality question (*Ibid.*).— About the importance of the years 1913-14 for the development of Lenin's thought on the nationality problem, see briefly Sorin, "Vladimir Iliich Lenin," (Lenin, *Selected Works,* I, 72) and G. H. Sabine, *A History of Political Theory* (N. Y., 1950), rev. ed., p. 846.

4. "On the Right of Nations to Self-Determination," *Soch.,* XVII, 437. While the "revival of national movements after 1905" is credited with having stimulated the "revival" of Bolshevik "agi-

tation" in the nationality field ("Discussion of Self-Determination Summed Up," *Soch.*, XIX, 271), the outbreak of the war had increased the significance of the question of nationality, "which was now tremendous" ("On the National Pride of the Great Russians," *Soch.*, XVIII, 80).

5. See Editors' Notes, *Soch.*, XIX, 241.

6. St. W. Page, "Lenin, the National Question, and the Baltic States, 1917-19," *The American Slavic and East European Review*, Feb. 1948, No. 1, p. 16.

7. There are numerous editions of the English version; see *Marxism and the National and Colonial Question* (N. Y., 1942).

8. See R. Pipes, *The Formation of the Soviet Union, 1917-1923* (Cambridge, 1954) and J. Towster, *Political Power in the U. S. S. R. 1917-47* (N. Y., 1948), especially chaps. iv and v.

9. L. Trotsky, *Stalin* (N. Y., 1941), pp. 156-57, was one of the first to point to Lenin's influence on Stalin in the latter's essay "Marxism and the National Question." Anyone examining the major writings of Lenin on this problem and Stalin's essay will have to confirm Trotsky's thesis; see also Madame N. K. Krupskaya's *Memories of Lenin* (transl. by E. Verney, N. Y., 1930), pp. 115-16, where she points to Lenin's guidance.

The best discussions in English of Lenin's thought on the nationality question may be found in B. D. Wolfe, *Three Who Made a Revolution* (N. Y., 1948), chap. 33, E. H. Carr, *op. cit.*, I, 410-28, espec. 418-28, J. Towster, *op. cit.*, espec. pp. 50-62, 80-81, 93-94, and R. Pipes, *op. cit.*, pp. 41-49. In their discussion of Bolshevik thought on nationality these authors deal, justifiably, in greater detail with Lenin's thought than with Stalin's. For a brief evaluation of Lenin's pertinent thought, see also H. Kohn, *Nationalism in the Soviet Union* (N. Y., 1933), pp. 43-48. There exists no detailed analysis of Lenin's thought on the nationality question in the Russian language. For a cursory discussion in Russian of this problem, see the Bibliography.

There has been a tendency in Stalin's Russia to exaggerate the originality and importance of Stalin's pamphlet *Marxism and the National Question*, while deemphasizing Lenin's greater theoretical contributions also in this field. The publication, for instance, of Stalin's essay on the national question is listed in the "Chronology of Principal Events" in the *History of the Communist Party of the Soviet Union. A Short History* (ed. W. Knorin [Moscow, 1935], p. 508), while none of Lenin's writings in this field are mentioned.

That this work, which originally appeared anonymously, was actually written by Stalin—and now forms volume XV of his *Sochineniia* (Moscow, 1946)—shows that the tendency of minimizing Lenin's theoretical importance in this field and of maximizing Stalin's was deliberately produced by Stalin himself. In sheer volume, aside from quality, Lenin's writings on the nationality question surpass by far those of Stalin in the pre-revolutionary period.

Yet the *Short History*, p. 143, devotes only five lines to Lenin and the national question, but gives to Stalin eighteen lines. Both Lenin and Stalin are credited with "developing theory," the first, "Marxist," the latter, "Bolshevik" theory, both with "exposing opportunist theories prevalent in the Second International." Lenin's theories are designated as of "greatest international importance," Stalin's of "exceptional importance." Lenin's role as the master, having a slight edge over the disciple, appears to be recognized in the reference to Stalin's "struggle for the Leninist line in the national question." Yet only Stalin is given credit for offering "detailed grounds for the national program of the Bolshevik Party," while in reality Lenin in his more elaborate essays of the period gives considerably greater attention to detailed questions of Bolshevik nationality policy.

Furthermore, casual praise of Stalin by Lenin in this respect is inflated beyond proportion. This laudatory remark was made by Lenin in the article "On the National Program of the R.S.D.L.P.," *Soch.*, XVII, 116: "In Marxian theoretical literature this state of affairs and the foundations of the national program of the Social Democrats have of late already been elucidated (here Comrade Stalin's article stands out prominently)." While praise in the parenthesis is stressed, another remark by Lenin, made in the same month, by implication critical of Stalin, has either escaped Stalin or, more likely, has been ignored or suppressed by him: "A popular brochure on the question of nationality is much needed." (Letter to Shaumian, Dec. 6, 1913, *Soch.*, XVII, 91). This was written only a few months after the publication of Stalin's essay "Marxism and the National Question" in *Prosveshcheniye* in March and April of 1913. The editorial notes on Stalin's work on the national question, *Sochineniia*, vol. II, contain only the more flattering remarks of Lenin. The same holds true of L. Beria's comments on Lenin's evaluation of Stalin's "Marxism and the National Question" in his work *On the History of the Bolshevik Organizations in Transcaucasia* (Moscow, 1949), pp. 776ff.

Had Lenin considered Stalin's contribution to the nationality question as the last word on this important problem, he would not have written as extensively on the national problem, and right after the publication of Stalin's essay, as he did. He also would have hardly induced another "Caucasian" comrade, namely Stepan Grigorevich Shaumian, to write a popular pamphlet on the nationality question in the Caucasus (see his letter of Aug. 11, 1913); concerning Lenin's correspondence with Shaumian on the nationality problem, see B. D. Wolfe, *op. cit.,* and *The Letters of Lenin,* transl. and ed. by E. Hille and D. Mudie (N. Y., 1953), especially pp. 327-28.

B. Wolfe, *op. cit.,* points likewise to the relegation of Lenin to a secondary role as a theoretician on the national question in the Stalinist era (587). Of the numerous essays of Lenin on the nationality problem, the Marx-Engels-Lenin Institute, preparing an edition of Lenin's *Selected Works* in the English language, had included a single essay of his, "On the Right of Nations to Self-Determination." This policy, however, is explained on the basis of Lenin's supposedly democratic convictions which had been embarrassing to the editors, and not, as appears more likely, in order to have Stalin's theoretical star shine brighter, undimmed by Lenin's greater brilliance.

10. See, for instance, "On the Right of Nations to Self-Determination," *Soch.,* XVII, 435-36.

11. E. Carr, *op. cit.,* I, 248.

12. N. K. Krupskaya, *Memories of Lenin* (London, 1930), pp. 184-85.

13. See Lenin's letter of Dec. 20, 1922, Trotsky Archive at Harvard University; quoted in full by R. Pipes, *The Formation of the Soviet Union* (Cambridge, 1954), p. 274.

14. *Pravda,* May 25, 1945.

15. *Address by Wladyslaw Gomulka to the Eighth Plenary Session of the Central Committee of the Polish United Workers Party,* Oct. 20, 1956 (Warsaw, 1956), p. 52. Immediately after this address, on October 30th—after the uprising in Hungary and Poland, and prior to the crushing of the Hungarian revolution by Russian troops—the government of the U.S.S.R. in an historic declaration on the "Principles of Development and Further Strengthening of Friendship and Cooperation between the Soviet Union and other Socialist States" (*Pravda,* Oct. 31, 1956; see P. E. Zinner, ed. *National Communism and Popular Revolt in Eastern Europe* [N. Y., 1956], pp. 485-89) referred specifically to the Twentieth Congress of the Communist Party of the Soviet Union in February,

1956, which had stressed the importance of the "Leninist principles of the equality of peoples in relation with the other socialist countries" (486). It was freely admitted in the Declaration that past "mistakes," "violations and errors" had "demeaned the principle of equality in the relations among socialist states" (486). This theme was taken up immediately, on November 1, 1956, and enthusiastically, by the government of the People's Republic of China in an official "Statement on the Declaration of the Soviet Government on Relations among Socialist States," which stressed that the relations between all nations, and "all the more so between socialist countries," should be based upon recognition also of "equality" (493-94). The leading Chinese communist organ, *People's Daily,* pointing likewise to the Soviet Russian government's Declaration, emphasized the current importance of "the Marxist-Leninist principle of equality of nationalities and the principle of proletarian internationalism" (491) and the Yugoslav *Borba* in an editorial of November 1st, commenting on the same document, similarly underlined the necessity of "consistent implementation of the Leninist principles of socialist internationalism" (495).

Long before, Sun Yat-sen, leader of the Kuomintang, wrote from his deathbed in March 1925 a letter to the Central Executive Committee of the U.S.S.R., extolling the "union of free republics" which he believed to be extant in the Soviet Union and "that heritage left to the oppressed peoples of the world by the immortal Lenin" (*New York Times,* May 24, 1925; quoted by H. Kohn, *Nationalism, Its Meaning and History,* 1955, pp. 184-85).

NOTES FOR CHAPTER ONE

For a more detailed description of the situation of the nationalities in Tsarist Russia, see Pipes, *op. cit.*

1. *Verhandlungen des Gesamtparteitages der Sozialdemokratie in Oesterreich (Bruenn)* (Vienna, 1899), pp. 74-75; for a criticism see O. Bauer, *Die Nationalitaetenfrage und die Sozialdemokratie,* in *Marxstudien,* vol. II (Vienna, 1924), pp. 527-28; this study appeared first in 1907.

2. *Verhandlungen des Gesamtparteitages* (. . .), p. 104.

3. According to K. Renner, *Das Selbstbestimmungsrecht der Nationen in besonderer Anwendung auf Oesterreich,* Part I, "Nation und Staat" (Vienna, 1918), the principle of personal autonomy

should supplement or take the place of territorial autonomy (pp. 71-75).—In the sixteenth century the territorial concept of *cuius regio, eius religio* had not established religious peace and equality. Likewise, in view of the nationally mixed character of the various regions and territories, the territorial principle is bound to lead not to equality of nations, but to national domination (1916, p. 75). The principle of personal autonomy separated the nationalities on the basis of individual preference and voluntary adherence to one or the other national group and extended to them legal recognition and national-cultural rights. The population had thus to be organized "twice," "once nationally and once according to administrative requirements. In either case the territorial units will be different" (K. Renner, *Grundlagen und Entwicklungsziele der oesterr.-ungarischen Monarchie* (Vienna, 1906), quoted by R. Kann, *The Multinational Empire, Nationalism and National Reform in the Habsburg Monarchy* [New York, 1950], II, 159). See also O. Bauer, *op. cit.*, on the principle of territorial autonomy, pp. 324-352, and the principle of personal autonomy, pp. 353-365.

4. Only if the nationalities will have secured the right of satisfying their cultural needs, O. Bauer, *op. cit.*, p. 314, insisted, will there be no further need "and desire to establish national parties"; no "national struggle" will then "paralyze the class struggle." L. Trotsky, in a brief comparison of Lenin's nationality policy with that of the Austrian socialists of whom he was highly critical, stressed that while the Bolsheviks, preparing for the seizure of power, anticipated and took into calculation the outbreak of national revolution, the Austrian Social Democracy was rather bent upon preserving Austria's polyglot empire (*History of the Russian Revolution,* III, 58-61). If the revolution, as Marx said, was the locomotive in history, then Austro-Marxism, Trotsky added, was its brake. The right to self-determination, to secession, was thus held to be a revolutionary slogan, an imperative of the "proletarian" revolution, and Austrian socialism was condemned because it did not wish to exploit the nationality question for immediate revolutionary purposes.

It is true that both Renner and Bauer wished to preserve the Austrian multinational state and to solve the national problem to pave the way for socialism in a large economic realm. (This is also the interpretation of K. Kautsky, "Nationalitaet und Internationalitaet," *Die Neue Zeit,* 1908, p. 23; see likewise R. A. Kann, *The Multinational Empire* (. . .), II, 167, as well as O. Jászi, *The Disso-*

lution of the Habsburg Monarchy [Chicago, 1929], pp. 177-84).
National culture and national endeavors were considered by both
writers to have intrinsic value, and the national problem was not
merely looked upon from the selfish and narrow tactical angle of
the Social Democratic Party and of the "proletarian" revolution.

Stalin's point of view, however, was similar to that of Trotsky.
Stalin expressed well the difference between the Austro-Socialist
and Russo-Bolshevik views of the nationality question when he
denied that, according to Leninism, the national problem could be
solved "off the high road of the proletarian revolution" (*Problemy
Leninizma,* Moscow, 1947, 11th ed., p. 47). It was only "formerly,"
prior to Lenin's exposition and analysis of the nationality question,
that the "reformist" had looked upon the national problem "as an
independent one having no connection with the general problems
of the rule of capital, of the overthrow of imperialism, of the proletarian revolution" (47). The latter had its own demands, and the
nationality problem in all its aspects had to be subordinated to it
and could only be solved within its framework. No independent
formulation of the national problem, no independent policy, was
feasible. Such "totalitarian" approach to the national problem was
indeed absent from the writings of Bauer and Renner.

5. Hromada means Community; Sakartvelo, Georgia; Dash-
naktsutiun, Federation.

6. Concerning the Bund see M. Rafes, *Ocherki po istorii
'Bunda'* (Moscow, 1923). G. Zinoviev, *Istoriia Rossiskoi Kommunisticheskoi Partii (b)* (Moscow, 1923), pays his respect to the revolutionary "heroism" of Jewish workers, but criticizes the emerging
"chauvinism" of the Bund (77-78). J. Martov, *Geschichte der
russischen Sozialdemokratie* (Berlin, 1926), pp. 64-66, is more
objective toward the Bund, yet stresses that its "political demand
aroused lively opposition among most Russian Social-Democratic
organizations" (65).

7. The Right, the Left, and the Center on the nationality
question did by no means always or fully correspond to the Right,
Left, and Center in the RSDRP generally. Until 1912 both Menshevik and Bolshevik writers rejected, for instance, federalism and
cultural autonomy, conspicuous points in the nationality program
of the Right and demanded by many socialists of the minority
peoples. Whatever their other theoretical differences, on the nationality question Mensheviks and Bolsheviks saw eye to eye. Yet the
increasing importance which Georgians and Jews and other national

minorities were to play in the Menshevik faction as well as the greater responsiveness of the Mensheviks to political democracy made this wing become reconciled to national-cultural autonomy, though not to federalism. A conference held in Vienna in August 1912, called by the Bolsheviks the conference of the "Liquidators," stressed that national-cultural autonomy was reconcilable with the Party's program of self-determination. In 1917 national-cultural autonomy became officially part of the Menshevik program (R. Pipes, *op. cit.*, p. 34; the position of the major Russian political parties on the national problem is here ably summarized, pp. 29-34). The Social Revolutionaries had come out for national-cultural autonomy as well as for federalism already at their first Congress. Nevertheless, the opposition to this program in the S. R. was strong and determined and thwarted any beneficial results which the adoption of these points might otherwise have had.

8. Though not opposed to national independence movements under all circumstances, Rosa Luxemburg had come to be looked upon by the left wing on the nationality question as representing true, uncompromising internationalism. In one of the earliest discussions of the national problem in socialist circles, Rosa Luxemburg, contrary to Marx's earlier approval of the Polish national independence movement, had opposed the Poles' right to self-determination. She had held that Poland in view of her close economic ties with Russia and the greater advantages also of a larger economic region should strive for an autonomous status within the frame of a democratic Russian state ("Die neuen Stroemungen in den polnischen sozialistischen Bewegungen in Deutschland und Osterreich," *Die Neue Zeit,* No. 32 and 33, 1896; also "Der Sozialpatriotismus in Polen," *ibid.,* No. 41, 1896). It was just over the nationality question and the future of Poland that Polish socialism split in the early 1890's when the national-minded Polish Socialist Party, the PPS, was born and the other group joined the RSDRP.

9. A Party resolution of the summer of 1913 acknowledged that the internal dissensions over the nationality question, "the attempt of the Caucasian Social Democrats, of the Bund, and of the Liquidators" to abolish the Party's nationality program had compelled the Party to give to this problem "even greater attention" (*Soch.,* XVII, 11). While the differences here referred to were with the Right, differences with the Left were no less serious. In regard to these differences Lenin admitted in 1916 that the discussion of the right to self-determination had revealed "some wavering of opinion

among members of our Party." This appears rather to understate his differences with the Left. On the next page Lenin frankly admitted: "The disagreement is fundamental" (XIX, 242). The importance of this discussion of the nationality question for the later nationality policy of the Soviet Union has been stressed by Lenin's widow, Madame Krupskaya, *Memoirs of Lenin* [London, 1930], pp. 184-85). The "underestimation of the right of nations to self-determination" by the Left, Krupskaya wrote, had "filled Vladimir Ilyich with indignation," while the "August bloc," which adopted the rightist view on the nationality question, was regarded by him as "opportunism" (183).

In the realm of pure theory Lenin apparently made more far-reaching concessions to nationalism than the Right. Conceding secession was a greater sacrifice from the point of view of the Great Russian proletariat than granting mere autonomy or even federalism. Yet the Right and many of the border nationalities seemed little interested in secession. Instead, the Right insisted on federalism and national-cultural autonomy, the very demands which Lenin then denied to Russia's various nationalities.

10. J. Maynard, *Russia in Flux* (N. Y., 1951), p. 458.

11. "On the Right of Nations to Self-Determination," *Soch.,* XVII, 458. The views of Marx on the nationality problem and on its solution have been ably discussed by S. F. Bloom in his work *The World of Nations. A Study of the National Implications of the Work of Karl Marx* (N. Y., 1941). Bloom reached the conclusion that "Marx, unlike some of his followers, did not believe in the principle of self-determination of nations" (33). He had especially distinguished "sharply" "between small and large nations in determining the right to separate statehood" (22).

12. The English version in *International Socialist Workers and Trade Union Congress* (London, 1896), p. 31, speaks of "autonomy," while the German version mentions "Selbstbestimmungsrecht" (*Verhandlungen und Beschluesse des Internationalen Arbeiter- und Gewerkschaftskongresses zu London* [Berlin, 1897], p. 18; see E. H. Carr, *op. cit.,* I, 417. Lenin refers continually to the German version (also XVII, 455). However, his interpretation of self-determination as right to secession is not warranted, not even on the basis of the German version.—Lenin's "Draft and Explanation of the Program of the Social-Democratic Party," written during the year 1895-96, contained a clause asking for "equal rights" for all nationalities (*Soch.,* I, 426), but did not yet include the

specific demand for the right to secession, not even to national self-determination.

13. Lenin approved wholeheartedly K. Kautsky's position on the nationality question which had prevailed at this Congress ("On the Right of Nations [. . .]," *Soch.*, XVII, 456). Kautsky's criticism of R. Luxemburg's view on the national question in general and that of Poland in particular had been expressed in the pages of *Die Neue Zeit* in 1896 ("Finis Poloniae," No. 42 and 43) and was a rejoinder to several articles published previously in the same journal by R. Luxemburg. Kautsky's position on this question at the Second Congress of the International was that Polish socialists should not be forbidden to raise the demand for the independence of Poland, but that the International as such ought not to be tied down to a definite stand at that time. What attracted Lenin to this view was no doubt its deliberate uncertainty and the tactical flexibility which it seemed to permit.

14. *VKP(B)* v. *Rezoliutsiiakh* (1950), pp. 11-14.

15. *VKP(B)*, I, 40.

16. "Resolution on the National Question," *Soch.*, XVII, 11; also *VKP(B)* I, 210-11. The editors of Lenin's Collected Works hold that all the articles on the nationality problem written by him after this Resolution were "in defense" of it (*Soch.*, XVII, 421).

17. See the editorial Notes, *Soch.*, XVII, 421; also Mme. Krupskaya, *Memoirs of Lenin*, p. 122.

18. "On the Right of Nations (. . .)," *Soch.*, XVII, 458.

NOTES FOR CHAPTER TWO

1. This view had already emerged in Lenin's early work *Who Are the Friends of the People?*—which was written in the spring and summer of 1894—the first in which Lenin touched upon the problem of nationality. Nationalism is seen here as a consequence of the industrial age and of the development of capitalism: "Since the leaders and masters of this process ['the growth of exchange between regions, the growth of commodity circulation'] were the merchant capitalists, the creation of these national ties was nothing but the creation of bourgeois ties" (*Soch.*, I, 73). "National sentiment" is no "factor independent" of the development of capitalism. The implication is clear: nationalism is a temporary phenomenon and will disappear with the victory of socialism.

M. Pavlovich, "Lenin i natsional'nii vopros," *Pod Znamenem Marksizma* (1924), p. 164, holds that Lenin in the foregoing work had "for the first time" come to grips with the nationality problem; see also Corliss Lamont, *Peoples of the Soviet Union* (N. Y., 1934), p. 164. Actually, Lenin just barely touches here on this question (*Soch.*, I, 71-74), though the few pages devoted to it disclose several ideas which are to form part of his permanent thought on the nationality question.

2. "Discussion (. . .) Summed Up," *Soch.*, XIX, 269.

3. "Critical Notes on the National Question," *Soch.*, XVII, 137-38.

4. *Nationalism*. A Report by a Study Group of Members of the Royal Institute of International Affairs (London, 1939) : "For Lenin the nation had no intrinsic value. It represented but an instrument in the struggle of the world proletariat for freedom and a transitional stage" (73) : see also pp. 72-75.

5. This, of course, also holds true of Marx. S. F. Bloom, *The World of Nations. A Study of the National Implications of the Work of Karl Marx* (N. Y., 1941), remarks that Marx "only very incidentally" was "a theorist of nationality or race" (18).

6. While Lenin makes the right to self-determination, to secession, the very center of his discussion of the nationality question, Stalin treats it rather briefly (*Marxism and the National and Colonial Question* [N. Y., 1942] pp. 23-24). Possibly influenced by Bauer's and Renner's writings—which he claimed to have refuted—Stalin accepted also the ideas of national character, of national psychology and national culture, while Lenin never speaks of national character and is sharply opposed to national culture, extolling international culture. R. Pipes, *op. cit.*, remarks aptly that Lenin's approach to nationality was "more negative" (40) than that of Stalin; the latter's attitude is even held to have been "positive."

7. Stalin, *op. cit.*, p. 12.

8. Resolution on the Question of Nationality, "Report and Resol. (. . .)" *Soch.*, XVII, 11-12.

9. "On the Right of Nations (. . .)," *Soch.*, XVII, 431-32; italics are Lenin's.

10. *Ibid.*, 432.

11. "Critical Notes (. . .)," *Soch.*, XVII, 139-40.

12. *Ibid.*

13. Rosa Luxemburg is at one time criticized because she had "lost sight of the most important thing, viz. the difference between

countries where the bourgeois-democratic reformation has long been completed" and those states where a democratic-bourgeois revolution had not yet taken place ("On the Right [. . .]," *Soch.,* XVII, 435-36.

14. *Ibid.,* 428; see also p. 431: "The best conditions for the development of capitalism are presented, undoubtedly, by the national state."

15. The Great Russian nationalism, Lenin holds, "is the most formidable at the present time" "precisely" because it is "less bourgeois and more feudal" (*Ibid.,* p. 440). The national state, Kautsky had rightly maintained, is the form of state "which corresponds most to present-day conditions (i.e. capitalist, civilized, economically progressive conditions as distinguished from medieval, pre-capitalist, etc.)."

16. *Ibid.,* 435.

17. *Ibid.,* 435-36.

18. On the one hand Lenin asserts that the West did not know any longer a national problem, since there were no multinational states in Western Europe. On the other hand, the national movement is held to be of great significance in the colonies. The West European powers, however, were colonial powers and were as much affected by colonial problems as the nationalities of the colonies. The nationality problem therefore existed in the West, taking there merely a different form.

19. "On the Right (. . .)," *Soch.,* XVII, 435-36; italics Lenin's.

20. *Ibid.*

21. *Ibid.,* 463-64.

NOTES FOR CHAPTER THREE

1. Resolution on the National Question, *Soch.,* XVII, 11; see also "On the Right (. . .)," *Soch.,* XVII, 428.

2. "A Caricature of Marxism," *Soch.,* XIX, 232; italics Lenin's.

3. The official interpretation of the slogan in the Stalinist era was the following: "Each nation had the right to secede from Russia and form an independent state. The Bolsheviks did not consider it absolutely [!] necessary that Russia be cut up into a great number of petty national states. But they were of the opinion that no one had the right forcibly to detain any particular nation within a unified Russian state." (*Communist Party of the Soviet Union. A Short History* [Moscow, 1935], p. 141).

4. As early as 1897 Lenin in the article "The Tasks of Russian Social Democrats" had stressed the "inseparable connection between *socialist* and *democratic* propaganda and agitation" and had emphasized that "revolutionary work in both spheres runs parallel" (*Soch.,* II, 176, italics A. D. L.'s). Self-determination is held by Lenin to be a "democratic" imperative for the international proletariat, a "revolutionary, consequently democratic" conception ("The Revolut. Prolet. and the Right of Nations to Self-Det.," *Soch.,* XVIII, 324), a "general-democratic" demand ("On the 'National-Cultural Autonomy,'" *Soch.,* XVII, 93); it is also basic for the immediate struggle for socialism, it is a proletarian, a socialist imperative (*Ibid.*).

It is difficult to avoid the conclusion that Lenin's thinking on the nationality question was decisively influenced by Karl Kautsky, who was greatly revered by Lenin prior to the outbreak of the War, but ruthlessly vilified by him thereafter. Lenin had often referred to K. Kautsky against O. Bauer and K. Renner. At the Stuttgart Congress of the Socialist International in 1907, Kautsky—in criticism of a motion made by a German fellow-socialist, Eduard David, which did not reject colonial policy under all circumstances—had pointed out that "democracy and socialist policy have nothing in common with conquest and foreign rule (. . .) If we want to exert a civilizing influence upon primitive peoples, the first prerequisite is to gain their confidence by granting them freedom (. . .). The sentence (proposed by David and the Commission) is at variance with all our socialist and democratic thinking." (*Internat. Soc. Cong. at Stuttgart, 1907* [Berlin, 1907], pp. 64-66). This could have been written word for word by Lenin! Like Kautsky, Lenin demands self-determination on the basis of both democracy and of socialism. He too continuously stresses the importance of gaining the "confidence" of the oppressed nationalities. Lenin appears to have read most carefully every one of Kautsky's not too numerous pages on the nationality question.

5. *Soch.,* XIII, 94.

6. "Tasks of Russian Social Democrats," *Soch.,* II, 177-78.

7. Resolution on the Question of Nationality, *Soch.,* XVII, 12.

8. Cf. Lenin, *State and Revolution, Soch.,* XXI, 382: "We are for the democratic republic as the best form of state for the proletariat under capitalism." See Sabine, *Hist. of Pol. Thought,* rev. ed. (N. Y., 1950), chap. 34, about Lenin's changing attitude to political democracy; according to Sabine, Lenin's appreciation of

political democracy as "the most advanced type of bourgeois state" (831) was still evident for a good part of the year 1917. Lenin seemed then to appreciate the advantages of political democracy for the fighting "proletariat" and for the Party and to prefer the road of bourgeois democracy to alternate routes leading to the proletarian dictatorship and to socialism. Bourgeois democracy is not valued by Lenin as such; it has rather an "instrumental function" and a "temporary" usefulness. See also H. B. Mayo, *Democracy and Marxism* (N. Y., 1955), p. 293—B. D. Wolfe, *op. cit.* pp. 291-92, is rather positive that democracy held sway over Lenin "until 1917"; his writings were "all full of such earnest avowals" of it that "there can be no doubt of their sincerity." Yet it rather appears that Lenin's appreciation of democracy was then largely based on narrow tactical considerations.

9. "The Revolutionary Proletariat (. . .)" *Soch.,* XVIII, 323-24; italics A. D. L.'s.

10. *Ibid.,* 324; italics Lenin's.

11. "On the Right of Nations (. . .)," *Soch.,* XVII, 438-39.

12. *Ibid.;* italics Lenin's.

13. *Ibid.;* italics Lenin's.

14. *Ibid.;* italics A. D. L.'s.

15. *Ibid.*

16. "The Revolutionary Proletariat (. . .)," *Soch.,* XVIII, 328.

17. "The Tasks (. . .)," *Soch.,* II, 176.

18. "The Socialist Revolution and the Right (. . .)," *Soch.,* XIX, 38.

19. "Discussion (. . .) Summed Up," *Soch.,* XIX, 277-79.

20. Resolution on the Question of Nationality, *Soch.,* XVII, 11.

21. "The Revolutionary Proletariat (. . .)," *Soch.,* XVIII, 328.

22. *Ibid.*

23. *Soch.,* I, 194.

24. *Soch.,* II, 176; italics Lenin's.

25. "The Socialist Revolution (. . .) Theses," *Soch.,* XIX, 38.

26. "On the Right of Nations (. . .)," *Soch.,* XVII, 456.

27. *Ibid.*

28. "The Socialist Revolution (. . .)," *Soch.,* XIX, 38.

29. *Ibid.,* 45.

30. *Ibid.,* 38.

31. "Discussion (. . .) Summed Up," *Soch.,* XIX, 259.

32. *Ibid.,* 262.

33.   "The Socialist Revolution (. . .)," *Soch.*, XIX, 46.

34.   *Ibid.*, 38.

35.   On one occasion Lenin goes even so far as to limit the significance of the slogan of national self-determination to the bourgeois-capitalist stage: "Interpreting the Marxian program in a Marxian and not a childish way, it is very easy to guess that it applies to bourgeois-democratic national movements." ("On the Right [. . .]," *Soch.*, XVII, 434-35.) At other times, however, Lenin specifically rejects the leftist view that self-determination ceases to be of importance after the "proletarian" revolution (See "A Caricature . . . ," *Soch.*, XIX, 220 and also "Discussion . . . ," XIX, 242).

36.   "On the National Pride," *Soch.*, XVIII, 80. Lenin referred here to Marx, according to whom no people that oppressed others could be free. See also "Socialism and War," *Soch.*, XVIII, 206: "The Socialists cannot reach their great aim without fighting against every form of national oppression."

37.   On one occasion Lenin points to an utterance of Friedrich Engels "Discussion (. . .)," *Soch.*, XIX, 266, quoted also in K. Kautsky, *Sozialismus und Kolonialpolitik* (Berlin, 1907), p. 19, according to which socialism demanded the right of formerly oppressed nationalities to self-determination: "The victorious proletariat," Engels had written in a letter of September 12, 1882, to Karl Kautsky, "can not impose its will on any alien nationality without thus undermining its own victory."

38.   "On the Right (. . .) to Self-determination," *Soch.*, XVII, 442.

39.   *Ibid.*, 441.

40.   *Ibid.*, 442.

41.   *Ibid.*

42.   See chaps. iv, "The Seizure of Power . . . " and v, "National Equality . . . " of this study.

43.   "On the Right (. . .)," *Soch.*, XVII, 442.

44.   *Ibid.*, 458.

45.   "Project for a Program of the Fourth Party Congress (. . .) Latvia," *Soch.*, XVII, 63; see also XVII, 465 and XIX, 41.

46.   "The Chinese War," *Soch.*, I, 63.

47.   "Reports and Resolutions (. . .)," *Soch.*, XVII, 458.

48.   "A Caricature (. . .)," *Soch.*, XIX, 218.

49.   "Discussion (. . .) Summed Up," *Soch.*, XIX, 262; italics Lenin's.

50. "On the Right of Nations (. . .)," *Soch.*, XVII, 442.

51. "Discussion (. . .)," *Soch.*, XIX, 267; italics A. D. L.'s.

52. "On the Right of Nations (. . .)," *Soch.*, XVII, 442; see also on Marx "educating" the English workers in internationalism, "The Socialist Revolution (. . .)," *Soch.*, XIX, 41-42.

53. "On the Right (. . .)," *Soch.*, XVII, 458; italics Lenin's. Lenin could not deny, however, that Bolshevik nationality policy strengthened nationalism to some degree.

54. "Critical Notes (. . .)," *Soch.*, XVII, 136.

55. *Ibid.;* italics Lenin's.

56. *Ibid.;* see also "Project for a Program (. . .)," *Soch.*, XVII, 66.

57. "Critical Notes (. . .)," *Soch.*, XVII, 137; see also "Project for a Program (. . .)," *Soch.*, XVII, 66.

58. "Critical Notes (. . .)," *Soch.*, XVII, 138.

59. *Ibid.*, 136.

60. E. H. Carr., *op. cit.*, I, 418.

61. The slogan of national-cultural autonomy "deceives the workers with the illusion of the cultural unity of the (. . .) nationality." "Project (. . .)," *Soch.*, XVII, 66. Lenin himself, though aware of the difference between national culture as such and the specific Austrian socialist project of national-cultural autonomy, rather tended to confuse them in order to discredit the Austrian program as an essentially bourgeois plan (*ibid.*). The slogan of national-cultural autonomy, Lenin asserted, is the program of "bourgeois nationalism."

62. See p. 23 of this study.

63. *Vtoroi S'ezd RSDRP* (1932), pp. 323-25; quoted by Carr, *op. cit.*, I, 419.

64. "Project (. . .)," *Soch.*, XVII, 66; italics Lenin's. In his writings on the nationality question Lenin, as pointed out, repeatedly makes critical reference to the Austrian socialists O. Bauer's and K. Renner's pertinent writings, relying often also on the authority of Karl Kautsky. The noted German socialist theoretician had given his major criticism of the works of the Austrian writers in "Nationalitaet und Internationalitaet" (*Die Neue Zeit*, Ergaenzungsheft, No. 1, Stuttgart, 1908). While Lenin is correct in holding that, in Kautsky's opinion, O. Bauer had "heavily exaggerated nationalism" (35), he overlooks that in another connection Kautsky gave "unstinted praise" (1) to both Renner and Bauer and that, in conclusion, he voiced the hope that a "federation of nationalities like the one which Bauer and Renner wished to make of Austria

will emerge from the states of Europe." "All ideas" expressed by the Austrian socialists, "all experiences" and "all" their "successes" are likely to help toward the "transformation of all of Europe, indeed of the entire circle of European culture" (36). Kautsky, very differently from Lenin, did not object to experimentation with the idea of national-cultural autonomy.

65. "On 'National-Cultural Autonomy,'" *Soch.*, XVII, 92-93.

66. *Ibid.*

67. "Project (. . .)," *Soch.*, XVII, 66; italics Lenin's.

68. Stalin, "Marxism and the National Question," *Soch.*, II, 365; or *Collected Works* (Moscow, 1953), II, 379.

69. *Soch.*, V, 248-49.

70. "The National Question in Our Program," *Soch.*, V, 344.

71. "To the Jewish Workers," *Soch.*, VIII, 24.

72. *Ibid.*

73. "Critical Notes (. . .)," *Soch.*, XVII, 141 and 143.

74. *Ibid.*, 141; italics Lenin's.

75. *Ibid.*, 140.

76. *Ibid.* After the October Revolution Lenin reversed himself on the question of the development of national culture. He who had opposed its development before 1917 "took a clear stand" thereafter "not only for autonomous cultural expression, but in favor of sustained aid for such" (J. Towster, *Political Power in the U. S. S. R. 1917-47*, p. 81). He came out "not only for real equality in rights, but also for the development of the language, the literature of the toiling masses of the formerly oppressed nations" (*Soch.*, 3rd ed., XXIV, 96; quoted by Towster, *op. cit.*, 81).

77. "Critical Notes (. . .)," *Soch.*, XVII, 142.

78. *Ibid.*, 143.

79. "Critical Notes (. . .)," *Soch.*, XVII, 141 and 143.

80. "On the 'National-Cultural Autonomy,'" *Soch.*, XVII, 93-94; on Lenin's unwillingness to "guarantee anything to any nation" see "On the Right (. . .)," *Soch.*, XVII, 439.

81. "Project for a Program (. . .)," *Soch.*, XVII, 67; this view, Lenin asserts, was the "undisputed judgment of undeniable experts of Jewish history": the authorities referred to, the socialist writers Otto Bauer and Karl Kautsky, would have hesitated to stake out such claims. Lenin bases his analysis of the situation of *Russia's* Jewry and his recommendations on the brief general observations of these two *Central-European* writers—with one of whom in regard to the nationality question he sharply disagreed.—At the

London Congress in 1903 Lenin had already denied that the Jewish people constituted a nationality (*Soch.*, VI, 84), had asserted that this conception was politically "reactionary" (84), that the Bund had in reality accepted "the zionist idea of a Jewish nationality" (86), and had maintained that the Jewish question was simply "assimilation or separation" (85); in rejecting the Bund's demand for federalism, Lenin was not only motivated by hostility to federalism and preference for centralism, but also by his opposition to "separation" and his favoring the assimilation and "amalgamation" of the Jews (VI, 80).

Stalin in his essay "Marxism and the National Question" (1913) criticized, like Lenin, the Bund not only for its demand for national-cultural autonomy, but also for its opposition to assimilation, on the ground that the existence of the Jewish nationality was still to be proven (*Marxism and the National and Colonial Question* [N. Y., 1942], p. 41).

82. "Critical Notes (. . .)," *Soch.*, XVII, 145; see also "The Revol. Prol. (. . .)," *Soch.*, XVIII, 325.

83. "Critical Notes (. . .)," Soch., XVII, 145; italics Lenin's. See also Lenin's letter to Gorki, written in the second half of February 1913, where he calls the joint organization of proletarians of different nationalities in the Caucasus "a proletarian solution of the national question," "the only solution."

84. See also "Critical Notes (. . .)," *Soch.*, XVII, 144, where Lenin pleads for common proletarian organizations embracing Great Russians and Ukrainians, and also Resolution on the National Question, *Soch.*, XVII, 12.

85. *Ibid.*, 140.

86. Such fear was expressed by the Left in the Party, leftist in regard to the nationality question, R. Luxemburg, Bukharin, Piatakov and others. Though Lenin hurled heavy ammunition against them, he regarded their position as not unsound in some respects, especially not in their emphasis on internationalism.

87. National hate would, according to Lenin, not vanish with the elimination of the class struggle. It was rather his view that national antipathies would disappear not after the "proletarian" seizure of power, but would persist for a long time, to vanish "only *after* the victory of socialism" ("Discussion [. . .] Summed up," *Soch.*, XIX, 267; italics Lenin's).

88. "Critical Notes (. . .)," *Soch.*, XVII, 146.

89. *Ibid.*, italics Lenin's.

90. *Soch.,* XVII, 154.

91. *Ibid.*

92. "Discussion (. . .) Summed Up," *Soch.,* XIX, 259.

93. "The Revolutionary Proletariat (. . .)," *Soch.,* XVIII, 325.

94. "Socialism and War. Attitude of the RSDLP Towards the War," *Soch.,* XVIII, 206.

95. "Revision of the Party Program," *Soch.,* XX, 295; italics A. D. L.'s. "We are no adherents of petty states," Lenin also wrote in 1917 in the article "The Ukraine" (XX, 535). It is just the unconditional recognition of the right of secession which alone makes possible a free "union of Ukrainians and Great Russians," "agitation" for a "voluntary [sic] union of both nationalities in one state" (534).

96. "The Revolutionary Proletariat (. . .)," *Soch.,* XVIII, 324.

97. "On the Right of Nations (. . .)," *Soch.,* XVII, 460.

98. *Ibid.*

99. Dvenadtsatyi s'ezd, 523 and 548; quoted by R. Pipes, *op. cit.,* p. 263.

100. Lenin stood often alone against a rather formidable opposition on the Left and on the Right. This at times solitary position of his on the nationality question was paralleled by a similar isolated position, for a good length of time, on several other important points of the Party program.

101. "On the Right of Nations (. . .)," *Soch.,* XVII, 460.

102. "Discussion (. . .) Summed Up," *Soch.,* XIX, 257.

103. It was also warped by political geography. While Lenin upheld the right of all nationalities to secession, the latter was technically possible only in the case of those nationalities which good fortune had placed geographically favorably, namely in the border regions. As far as the nationalities of the interior were concerned, self-determination, narrowly conceived as secession and not including the right to federalism or autonomy, was definitely limited. All that was held out to these nationalities was elimination of discrimination and equality irrespective of national origin. Also, the promise was given that autonomy would be granted, though the national minority had no right to demand it.

104. Such "tactical" decisions, which often were bound to decide the fate of small nationalities, were obviously to be made by the unitary Party in which the Bolsheviks of the nationality concerned were in a hopeless minority. See chap. iv of this study: "Self-Determination and Implementation."

105. "Discussion (. . .) Summed Up," *Soch,* XIX, 264.

106. *Ibid.,* 328-29; as early as 1903 Lenin had denied that the Party program, apparently "not quite clear to some people," obligated the Party to the support of self-determination in every case ("The Nat. Progr. [. . .]," *Soch.,* V, 337).

107. "Discussion (. . .)," *Soch.,* XIX, 260-61.

108. "On the Right (. . .)," *Soch.,* XVII, 438-39.

109. "The Socialist Revolution (. . .)," *Soch.,* XIX, 42; see also "A Caricature (. . .)," *Soch.,* XIX, 219.

110. "On the Right (. . .)," *Soch.,* XVII, 438-39.

111. *Ibid.*

112. *Ibid.,* 440.

113. "On the National Pride (. . .)," *Soch.,* XVIII, 80.

114. "Socialism and War (. . .)," *Soch.,* XVIII, 195.

115. "On the Right (. . .)," *Soch.,* XVII, 428.

116. "A Caricature (. . .)," *Soch.,* XIX, 198; see also *Soch.,* XVIII, 194.

117. "Discussion (. . .)," *Soch.,* XIX, 249.

118. *Ibid.,* 254.

119. *Ibid.,* 251; italics Lenin's.

120. "Socialism and War (. . .)," *Soch.,* XVIII, 206-07.

121. "The Socialist Revolution (. . .) Theses," *Soch.,* XIX, 30.

122. *Ibid.,* 40; see also XVIII, 324. It is apparently passages like these which prompted B. D. Wolfe in his generally penetrating book *Three Who Made a Revolution* (N. Y., 1948) to write that Lenin had stood for "no socialism without democracy" and to extol "Lenin the democrat." His "articles on the national question and imperialism" were "filled with this democratic spirit" (587). For a rejection of this view, see the chap. "Self-Determination and Its Implementation" in this study.

123. This point is also made in the "Theses on the International Situation and the Policy of the Entente," adopted by the Founding Congress of the Communist International in March, 1919, which condemn the Entente on account of the denial of national self-determination to Germany, Austria, and Hungary, all losers of the War; these states were looked upon in the spring of 1919 as the most fertile field for communist propaganda and the most promising target of Soviet Communism (*Kommunisticheskii Internatsional,* No. 1, May 1919, p. 113; see also A. D. Low, *Austria Between Two Soviet Republics. In the Mirror of the Russian Press of 1919* [1956], p. 53, unpublished manuscript, The Russian

Institute, Columbia University). These vanquished states, while not colonial and not politically dependent, were considered "oppressed" nations, though the "oppression" is here rather of international than of national scope. What was then propagated was an alliance between the proletariat of the former oppressor nationality, the Great Russian proletariat, not only with the national liberation movements of the colonies and dependent nationalities, but also with the just vanquished nations which "were broken by the war and shattered in their foundations."

124. This idea of the alliance between the proletariat and oppressed nationalities (Stalin stresses the importance for the proletariat of the "thesis" of the "possibility of a united front" between the two movements, "Questions Concerning the History of Bolshevism," *Leninizm,* 1954, p. 390) is more fully developed on pp. 78-82 of this study.

125. Stalin's interpretation that Leninism "broke down the wall between Europeans and Asiatics, between the 'civilized' and 'uncivilized' slaves of imperialism and thus linked the national problem with the problem of colonies" (*Problemy Leninizma,* 1952, eleventh ed., pp. 46-54) is essentially correct, though Lenin was hardly original in this regard. Other Marxist writers, especially Rudolf Hilferding, *Das Finanzkapital* (Vienna, 1910) and Herman Gorter, *Der Imperialismus, der Weltkrieg und die Sozialdemokratie.* Transl. from the Dutch (Amsterdam, 1915) had closely analyzed imperialism and had also stressed its impact upon nationalism and the proletariat.

126. "Discussion (. . .)," *Soch.,* XIX, 247; see also 262.

127. *Ibid.,* 247.

128. *Ibid.,* 142.

129. *Ibid.;* italics Lenin's.

130. "Socialist Revolution (. . .)," *Soch.,* XIX, 41.

131. L. Trotsky, *The History of the Russian Revolution* (N. Y., 1932), III, 38 and 61; revealingly, he uses this word twice in different contexts: "Only in this way [by espousing the slogan of national self-determination]," he writes, "could the Russian proletariat gradually win the confidence of the oppressed nationalities" (38); see also III, 61: "This bold revolutionary formulation of national problems won for the Bolshevik Party the indestructible confidence of the small and oppressed people of Tsarist Russia." In June, 1917, Lenin, pleading for autonomy of the Ukraine, stressed that such a concession by the Provisional Government would pave

the way to "mutual confidence between both nationalities," Great Russians and Ukrainians ("The Ukraine and the Defeat of Russian Governmental Parties," *Soch.*, XX, 541). There are few words which appear with as great frequency in the official Party statements and Lenin's writings on the nationality question as the word "confidence."

132. See also Merle Fainsod, *How Russia Is Ruled* (Cambridge, 1953), pp. 57-58.

NOTES FOR CHAPTER FOUR

1. "A Caricature (. . .)," *Soch.*, XIX, 220; italics Lenin's.
2. *Ibid.*, 221; italics Lenin's.
3. *Ibid.*
4. "Discussion (. . .)," *Soch.*, XIX, 268.
5. "The Socialist Revolution (. . .)," *Soch.*, XIX, 39; italics A. D. L.'s.
6. "A Caricature (. . .)," *Soch.*, XIX, 221; italics Lenin's. The interpretation of Lenin's view given by Stalin in early April, 1924, in his lectures "The Foundations of Leninism" which he delivered at Sverdlov University, was basically correct. "Formerly," he wrote, "it was tacitly assumed that the victory of the proletariat in Europe was possible without a direct alliance with the liberation movement in the colonies, that the national-colonial problem could be solved (. . .) off the highroad of the proletarian revolution." Indeed, Lenin made at times not only the proletarian victory dependent on the uprising of the oppressed peoples, but also the victory of the latter contingent upon the success of the proletariat of the oppressor nationality. A denial of the importance of this connection between the proletarian revolution and national-colonial revolution is branded by Stalin as representing an "anti-revolutionary point of view" which Lenin had already definitely "exposed" (Stalin, *Problemy Leninizma*, 1947, p. 47). See also M. Pavlovich, "Lenin i natsional'nyi vopros," *Pod Znamenem Marksizma*, 164-188, especially 183: "Lenin showed" that without a correct policy in the nationality question "the proletariat will not succeed in overthrowing the rule of the bourgeoisie and in bringing about the social revolution." Lenin's "Additions to the Theses on the National and Colonial Question," adopted at the Congress in 1921 are quite in line with these earlier views: "The separation of the colonies and the proletarian revolution will overthrow the capitalist order in Europe" (*Soch.*, XXV, 573).

"For the complete success of the world revolution a cooperation of both forces is needed."

7. "Discussion (. . .)," *Soch.,* XIX, 269.

8. *Ibid.;* italics Lenin's.

9. *Ibid.,* 270.

10. *Ibid.,* 255.

11. *Ibid.,* 270.

12. *Ibid.*

13. *Ibid.;* italics Lenin's.

14. "Discussion (. . .)," *Soch.,* XIX, 256.

15. In his letter to Shaumian of Dec. 6, 1913 Lenin wrote: "The advantages of the large state are above doubt." *Soch.,* XVII, 89-90.

16. "Discussion," 256.

17. *Ibid.,* 262.

18. See p. 33 of this study.

19. "A Caricature (. . .)," *Soch.,* XIX, 219.

20. "The Revolutionary Proletariat (. . .)," *Soch.,* XVIII, 327.

21. "Discussion (. . .)," *Soch.,* XIX, 262.

22. *Ibid.;* italics Lenin's.

23. "Socialism and War (. . .)," *Soch.,* XVIII, 206; italics Lenin's.

24. "The Socialist Revolution (. . .)," *Soch.,* XIX, 37.

25. *Soch.,* XVII, 89-90.

26. "The Socialist Revolution (. . .)," *Soch.,* XIX, 39.

27. Lenin holds it "absurd" to speak of a " 'right of nations to federation' " ("On the Right [. . .]," *Soch.,* XVII, 464). Federalism is considered "harmful" ("The National Question [. . .]," *Soch.,* V, 343-44). See the chap. "Federalism and Autonomy" in this study.

28. The Revolutionary Proletariat (. . .)," *Soch.,* XVIII, 325.

29. The centralized unitary state does, of course, not grant the right to secede to the population of any part of its territory. There is today a clear contradiction between the Soviet Constitution giving "freedom" of separation to the border republics, the border nationalities (see Article 17 of the Soviet Constitution in S. N. Harper and R. Thompson, *The Government of the Soviet Union,* secd. ed. [N. Y., 1949], p. 332), and the Party's Constitution and practice prohibiting agitation for secession ("Ustav kommunisticheskoi partii sovetskogo soyuza" [The Rules of the Communist Party of the Soviet Union], *Pravda,* Oct. 14, 1952; it is the duty

of the Party member to "guard the unity of the Party in every way."
It is evident that the pertinent Soviet constitutional provision, a
theoretical heritage of the past, of Lenin's and the Party's earlier
pronouncements, is purely illusory, while the Party's Constitution
expresses the reality of Soviet and the national minorities' existence.
Asserting the right of the national border republics to secession, the
Soviet Constitution also attaches no time limit to this privilege.
It simply abounds in generosities; not so Lenin prior to 1917, as a
closer analysis reveals.

In his report to the Tenth Congress of the Russian Communist
Party Stalin observed: "Inasmuch as the Soviet states join in the
federation voluntarily, the right to secession remains unavailed of
because the peoples that form the RSFSR have themselves so
willed" (*Marxism and the National and Colonial Question* [N. Y.,
1942], p. 106). They are apparently not permitted to change their
mind and leave the Union. This position of Stalin is fully in accord
with Lenin's view of the nationality problem at the time under discussion, but gives the lie to Article 17 of the Soviet Constitution
which "permits" secession.

30. "Liberated from the yoke of the bourgeoisie," the proletariat
of the former oppressed nationalities will strive "with all its might
to ally" itself "with the great advanced socialist nations" ("Discussion (. . .)," *Soch.*, XIX, 256).

31. Letter to Shaumian, Dec. 6, 1913, *Soch.*, XVII, 89-90.

32. "The Socialist Revolution (. . .)," *Soch.*, XIX, 39.

33. "On the National Program (. . .)," *Soch.*, XVII, 119.

34. "The Revolutionary Proletariat (. . .)," *Soch.*, XVIII, 324.

35. *Ibid.*

36. "Discussion (. . .)," *Soch.*, XIX, 256; italics A.D.L.'s.

37. To the Jews, and in particular to the Bund which was
Marxist and had become also Jewish-national-minded, though not
Zionist—Lenin's formula of national self-determination with its
narrow interpretation, the right to secession, appeared rather
meager. The Jews were in no position to invoke the right to secession. Geography, their dispersion, made such rights illusory
for them. The Bundists' demand for national-cultural autonomy
grew out of their desire to secure means to maintain the Jews'
existence as a nationality. Lenin bitterly opposed extraterritorial
autonomy not only for organizational reasons, but also since it
would counteract a natural process, the assimilation of the Jews.
About assimilation of the Jews, see p. 62 of this study; about

national-cultural autonomy, pp. 55-59; about autonomy, pp. 107-109.

38. "Resolution on the National Question (. . .)," *Soch.* XVII, 11-13.

39. "On the National Program (. . .)," *Soch.,* XVII, 119; italics Lenin's.

40. "The Socialist Revolution (. . .)," *Soch.,* XIX, 37.

41. "On the National Program (. . .)," 119.

42. *Ibid.*

43. "Discussion (. . .)," *Soch.,* XIX, 244.

44. "Resolution on the National Question (. . .)," *Soch.,* XVII, 11-13; see also "On the Right (. . .)," *Soch.,* XVII, 440-41: The proletariat "evaluates every national demand, every national separation, from the angle of the class struggle of the workers."

45. "On the National Program (. . .)," *Soch.,* XVII, 119.

46. *Soch.,* VI, 18-20.

47. *Ibid.* 19; in another connection Lenin speaks of "treachery to socialism" ("The Socialist Revolution [. . .]," *Soch.,* XIX, 37) which, it is understood, the Party is not going to commit.

48. "Speech on the Question of the Position of the Bund (. . .)," *Soch.,* VI, 19; italics Lenin's.

49. "On the Right (. . .)," *Soch.,* XVII, 438; italics Lenin's.

50. See paragraph 18 of the Party Rules, quoted by Hill-Stoke-Schneider, *The Background of European Governments* (N. Y., 1951), p. 326.

51. *Soch.,* XVII, 90; italics Lenin's.

52. Lenin demanded, for instance, the subordination of the interests of small nationalities to large ones, the subordination of the self-determination of even large nationalities to the interests of the proletariat and of socialism; he also favored the assimilation of individuals and groups dispersed throughout Russia rather than their cultural development.

53. "The Socialist Revolution (. . .)," *Soch.,* XIX, 41.

54. "On the Right (. . .)," *Soch.,* XVII, 441.

55. *Ibid.,* 463.

56. *Soch.,* XIX, 238.

57. "On the Right (. . .)," *Soch.,* XVII, 440; italics Lenin's.

58. This nationality "policy" was indeed applied by the Bolsheviks after the seizure of power. Whenever possible, they imposed their rule; where circumstances forbade this course, they "granted" independence.

59. Mme. Krupskaya, *Memories of Lenin* (London, 1930), p. 183.

60. Riazanov called Lenin during the debates on the nationality question at the Eighth Party Congress in 1919 "our old opportunist" (quoted by W. V. Harpe, *Die Grundsaetze der Nationalitaetenpolitik Lenin's* (. . .) [1941], p. 87).

61. "On the National Pride," *Soch.,* XVIII, 82.

62. "The National Question (. . .)," *Soch.,* V, 344.

63. *Ibid.,* 343-44.

64. "On the Position of the Bund (. . .)," *Soch.,* VI, 18.

65. "At the Occasion of the Declaration of the Bund," *Soch.,* V, 243.

66. "The National Question (. . .)," *Soch.,* V, 337.

67. "On the Right (. . .)," *Soch.,* XVII, 463-64.

68. *Soch.,* XVII, 89-90; italics Lenin's.

69. *Ibid.;* see here also Lenin's remarks: "We are against federalism."

70. "The Revolutionary Proletariat (. . .)," *Soch.,* XVIII, 325.

71. *Soch.,* XVII, 89-90.

72. "On the Right (. . .)," *Soch.,* XVII, 464.

73. In *Problemy Leninizma* (1947), p. 46, Stalin wrote: "Formerly, the principle of self-determination of nations was usually misinterpreted, and not infrequently it was narrowed down to the idea of the right of nations to autonomy." "Leninism broadened the conception of self-determination and interpreted it as the right (. . .) to complete secession." Actually, genuine self-determination includes not only the right to secession, but also the right to federalism and to autonomy. Thus, the nationality which rejects secession does not remain standing empty-handed.—Lenin, far from "broadening" the conception of self-determination, arbitrarily "narrowed" it down, so much as to leave the nationalities nothing but the right to secession; this "right" was further emaciated by numerous qualifications which he attached to it. E. H. Carr, *The Bolshevik Revolution 1917-23,* calls aptly Lenin's position, giving the nationalities the right to secession, but denying their right to virtually anything else, an "all or nothing" position (I, 420). Lenin gave the nationalities the alternative of complete separation or complete submission, complete freedom or "voluntary" acceptance of the whip. The nationalities which neither could nor would secede were faced with a harsh, brutally stiff ultimatum. This alternative was not a real freedom of choice.

74. "Project for a Program (. . .)," *Soch.*, XVII, 65; see also "On the Right (. . .)," *Soch.*, XVII, 463-64: "As far as autonomy is concerned, Marxists defend not the right to autonomy but autonomy *itself*, as a general, universal principle of a democratic state with a mixed national composition, with sharp differences in the geographical and other condition" (Italics Lenin's). Lenin does not object to "regional," to territorial autonomy (see also Stalin, *Marxism and the Nat. and Colon. Question* [N. Y., 1942], p. 73 where he speaks out for "regional autonomy"). This, of course, is not national-cultural autonomy, which is a personal rather than a territorial autonomy (see pp. 23-24 of this study). Lenin's autonomy happens also to be one which is granted by the central authorities and which may be withdrawn by them any time.

75. In rejecting federalism, Lenin denied the border nationalities constitutional guarantees and indirectly raised a serious threat to their continued existence. The Austrian socialist and theoretician of nationality Otto Bauer, on the other hand, emphasized in his work *Die Nationalitaetenfrage* (. . .) (1924) the importance of "securing" to the nationalities the "power" to "satisfy their cultural needs" (314). The proletariat of all nationalities must demand such a "regulation" of the nationality problem that "each nation has the opportunity of a steady cultural development" (317) and is to receive a "constitution" guaranteeing to it this and other rights (318-19).

This difference between Lenin and O. Bauer in their approach to the nationality question is characteristic and revealing in more than one respect, not only in regard to the genuineness of their respective desires to solve the nationality problem on the democratic basis of self-determination, but also in regard to their respective conceptions of constitutionalism and limitation of power. Bauer's conception is that of the Western rule of law, Lenin's that of the unfettered government of the Party claiming to rule in the interests of the people, more exactly of the "working" people. Lenin and the Bolsheviks spurned the idea of constitutional limitations of the sovereign power. Cf. M. Fainsod, *op. cit.*, p. 291: "The conception of constitutionalism is alien to the Soviet Union."

76. *Soch.*, XVII, 90; italics Lenin's.

77. "The Socialist Revolution (. . .)," *Soch.*, XIX, 40; on "democratic centralism" and autonomy, see also "Critical Notes (. . .)," *Soch.*, XVII, 54-55. See also pp. 97 and 101-102 of this study.

78. "Project for a Program (. . .)," *Soch.*, XVII, 67; see Party Rules quoted by Hill-Stoke-Schneider, *The Background of European Governments* (N. Y., 1951), especially p. 326.

79. "The Socialist Revolution (. . .)," *Soch.*, XIX, 39; italics Lenin's.

80. *Soch.*, XVII, 89-90.

81. "Resolution (. . .)," *Soch.*, XVII, 12.

82. Lenin's rejection of federalism in these pre-revolutionary writings contrasts sharply with the adoption later of the principle of federalism by the Communists and its being woven into the very fabric of the Soviet state. Article 13 of the Constitution of the U. S. S. R. refers to the Union of Soviet Socialist Republics as a "federal state, formed on the basis of a voluntary union of equal Soviet Socialist Republics," and Article 17 assures to every Union Republic "the right freely to secede from the U. S. S. R." (S. N. Harper and R. Thompson, *The Government of the Soviet Union,* secd. ed. [N. Y., 1949], p. 332).

As has been noticed, the idea of a voluntary union of the nationalities in the proletarian multinational state, the idea of the equality of all nationalities, and the right of secession were extolled by Lenin. It is these ideas which have found expression in the foregoing articles of the Constitution of the U. S. S. R.

The conception of federalism has likewise taken form in the Constitution of the Soviet Union. In striking contrast, however, to the above mentioned ideas, Lenin prior to 1917 had not only not supported federalism, but had sharply criticized it.

It is, of course, true that Soviet federalism, in view of the centralistic structure of the Communist Party apparatus and of Soviet centralized planning, is in some regards rather a myth than reality (M. Fainsod, *How Russia Is Ruled* [Cambridge, 1953], pp. 291-327). Soviet theory and practice have tended to diverge in regard to federalism. Nevertheless, the theoretical turnabout of Lenin and the Bolsheviks on the question of federalism versus centralism in the early post-war period stands out as an event of great theoretical and some practical significance.

The forces responsible for this change of Lenin's and of Soviet thought on federalism in the days after the October Revolution and in the Civil War do not concern us here. The explanation for Lenin's "reversal" (J. Towster, *Political Power in the U. S. S. R. 1917-1947* [N. Y., 1948], p. 62) was simply that the Party, facing after the seizure of power unexpectedly strong national movements, proposed federation not for its own sake, but as the best means to block separation. This has been openly admitted by Andrei Vyshinsky, *The Law of the Soviet State,* transl. by H. W. Bobb [N. Y., 1948]. The Party, he wrote, "put forward federation as a means of holding the masses of nationalities in the camp of the proletarian revolution" (224). See also E. H. Carr, *op. cit.,* I, chaps. x-xiv.

83.   "The National Question (. . .)," *Soch.,* V, 337.

84.   "The Socialist Revolution (. . .)," *Soch.,* XIX, 40.

85.   See also "The Revol. Prolet. (. . .)," *Soch.,* XVIII, 325, italics Lenin's, where Marx is quoted as an opponent of the federation principle; yet he had considered "the secession of an oppressed nation a step towards federation, consequently, not towards the splitting of nations, but towards concentration." This was Lenin's viewpoint also at a later period, in March, 1918: "Even federation (. . .), if it is established within bounds that are reasonable from the economic point of view (. . .), does not in the least contradict democratic centralism. Time and again, given a real democratic order, a federation (. . .) constitutes only a transitional step to a really democratic centralism (*Soch.,* third ed., XXII, 415-16; quoted by J. Towster, *op. cit.,* p. 63). Federalism is not looked upon statically, but rather constitutes a stepping stone leading to "concentration," to "democratic centralism."

NOTES FOR CHAPTER FIVE

1.   "A Caricature (. . .)," *Soch.,* XIX, 224.

2.   Lenin follows here apparently Marx's and Engels' views as expressed in *Manifest der kommun. Partei, in Marx-Engels Gesamtausgabe,* ed. V. Adoratskii, 1. Abt., vol. 6: "The bourgeoisie has through its exploitation of the world market given a cosmopolitan character to production and consumption in every country (. . .) In place of the old local and national seclusion and self-sufficiency, we have intercourse in every direction, universal inter-dependence of nations. And as in material, so also in intellectual production. The intellectual creations of individual nations become common property. National one-sidedness and narrow-mindedness become more and more impossible, and from the numerous national and local literatures there arises a world literature" (529). "National differences and antagonisms between peoples are vanishing gradually from day to day, owing to the development of the bourgeoisie (. . .)." "The supremacy of the proletariat will cause them to vanish still faster" (543).

3. "Discussion (. . .)," *Soch.*, XIX, 245; italics Lenin's.

4. *Ibid.*, 267.

5. *Ibid.;* italics Lenin's. The same idea was expressed in 1920 in the "Theses on the National and Colonial Question," adopted by the Second Congress of the Communist International, in which it was said that the "lack of confidence in the oppressor nationalities" and also in the "proletariat of these nationalities" can "vanish" only after the elimination of imperialism and after a radical change of the economic foundation of life in the leading and backward countries. Therefore, the "dying away of these prejudices will take place only slowly" and will require of the proletariat "special consideration" and a readiness to make "certain concessions" (*Kommunisticheskii Internatsional v dokumentakh 1919-32,* ed. Béla Kun, Moscow, 1933, pp. 129-30).

A comparison of Lenin's views on the tempo of the disappearance of national antipathies with those of Marx and Engels, especially as expressed in the *Communist Manifesto,* reveals a difference of some significance. Marx and Engels wrote thus: "In proportion as the antagonism between classes within the nation vanishes, the hostility of one nation to another will come to an end" "National antagonisms" will "vanish" during the period of the "supremacy of the proletariat" (*op. cit.,* 543). Lenin rather pointed to the considerable obstacles to real understanding between nationalities which will "not quickly vanish"; they will vanish "only *after* the victory of socialism," not, as Marx seemed to believe, during the proletarian dictatorship, during "the supremacy of the proletariat." That this was Lenin's view, was also held by the study group of the Royal Institute of International Affairs, *Nationalism* (London, 1939), p. 73.

6. See pp. 60-64 of this study.

7. "Critical Notes (. . .)," *Soch.*, XVII, 146.

8. In his book "Who are the Friends of the People?", *Soch.*, I, Lenin had stressed already the importance of "organizing and uniting the oppressed class for a struggle against the oppressor class in each separate country" and of "*amalgamating* such national working-class organizations into a single working-class army" (p. 74; italics A. D. L.'s).

9. Karl Kautsky, to whom Lenin prior to the War repeatedly referred as against the Austrian socialist theoreticians of nationality, K. Renner and O. Bauer, appealed to Lenin on account of his criticism of the nationality policy of the Austrian socialists, espe-

cially of their concept of extraterritorial national-cultural autonomy, and on account of his belief in the likely assimilation of many a nationality, while Renner and Bauer held that nationalism was rather on the increase.

Kautsky criticized also, as later Lenin and Stalin did, Bauer's definition of nationality, a definition which stressed national character rather than language. "There is thus no German nationality," Kautsky, sums up incredulously, "which comprises the entire nation. Will we ever have a chance to see one? By no means if its existence depends on a 'unified unique character'." ("Nationalitaet und Internationalitaet," *Die Neue Zeit,* Ergaenzungsheft, No. 1 [1908], 12). The German socialist, preferring to see Germany as an ethnically homogenous state, sensed in Bauer's conception of nationality an obstacle to German national unity and preferred to base nationality upon language; "unfortunately," Bauer had not "sufficiently" appreciated "the importance of language" "for the nationality as well as for the state" (22). A change of language is easier than a change of character, and thus assimilation of groups which are based primarily upon common language speedier. "Where everyone speaks two languages, one of these will ultimately be generally preferred on whatever ground—perhaps it is the language of the wealthier or more powerful nationality or because it offers a more developed literature." This was precisely Lenin's view —and his hope. Both "internationalists," Kautsky and Lenin, counted on the victory of the German, respectively the Great Russian, language over languages of smaller, less powerful, and, economically and culturally, less developed nationalities; both looked forward to the assimilation of smaller ethnic groups.

10.   "Critical Notes (. . .)," *Soch.,* XVII, 143-44; italics A. D. L.'s.

11.   Cosmopolitanism, so much vilified in the U. S. S. R. during the last decade, has become an object of derision and slander in the Soviet vocabulary. It has acquired the connotation of rootlessness and admiration of everything foreign, and has come to signify lack of patriotism. Yet Lenin was clearly a cosmopolitan. He always approved assimilation, opposed national culture, and denied, at least prior to 1917, that it was the proletariat's task to develop the culture of all nationalities.

In denouncing cosmopolitanism, Stalin and the Soviet leaders have preferred to overlook Lenin's position on this question. In spite of the recent revival of Leninism, it is of interest to note that the struggle against cosmopolitanism has merely abated, but not ceased.

12.   *Soch.*, XVII, 89-90; italics A. D. L.'s.

13.   S. F. Bloom, discussing Marx's views on the nationality problem in his work *The World of Nations* (N. Y., 1941) concludes that, according to Marx, "there is room for variety in the world, even if its economic systems should approach uniformity" (32). Marx "was decidedly not a cosmopolite in his picture of world order, although there were many traces of cosmopolitanism in his thought" (207). It would appear that Lenin pictured an ultimate communist order which showed a considerably less variegated national complexion than that of Marx.

14.   It is also Stalin's view, expressed by implication and some-times directly, that Lenin envisioned ultimate fusion and amalga-mation of nationalities. This carries special significance since Stalin was more set upon developing national cultures than upon assimi-lation and ethnic amalgamation. Stalin rejected the attempts of those in the Party who wished to embark upon the road leading to Lenin's cosmopolitan rather than international goal immediately, at the concrete historical stage in which Soviet Russia found herself in the late twenties and early thirties. In his report to the Sixteenth Congress of the Communist Party of the Soviet Union in 1930, Stalin, in a discussion of deviations in the nationality question, referred to the Great Russian chauvinist deviation; according to it, victory of socialism meant "fusing of nations into a single whole" *(Marxism and the National and Colonial Question* [N. Y., 1942], p. 203) and converting their national languages into a single common language, and demanded the "renunciation" of the "policy of fostering the development of the national culture of formerly oppressed peoples." The deviationists, Stalin pointed out, "usually refer to Lenin, misquoting him, and sometimes directly distorting and slandering him." According to Stalin, this "Great Russian chauvinist" deviation was the more "dangerous," since it held that the time had arrived to put "in the interest of internationalism" an end to the national republics and regions and propagated a "policy of assimilation."

On this occasion Stalin pointed out that Lenin's position was by no means that of the "deviationists," but, to the contrary, in line with his own stand and that of the majority of the Party. A careful reading of Stalin's line of argumentation reveals, however, that he himself did not object to a fusion of national cultures and languages in the distant future, but merely held in 1930 that "the demand for the abolition of national republics and regions in the present period of history" was "a reactionary demand" (206). According to Lenin, Stalin held, national differences among peoples "will continue to exist for a very long time even after the dictatorship of the proletariat has been established on a world scale," and a fusion of languages "into one common language" will likewise not occur for a very long time to come. Stalin does not deny here that cosmopolitanism rather than internationalism, the latter being based upon the continued existence of ethnic and linguistic entities, was Lenin's and, by implication, also his and the Party's ultimate goal.

This also becomes evident when Stalin, immediately after the foregoing, raised the question of a possible contradiction between the Party's policy of furthering national cultures and its ultimate goal of uniformity rather than diversity of national cultures—not merely in content, but also in form—and flatly denied that any contradiction existed. There was "nothing strange," Stalin maintained, in permitting the nationalities to develop and to expand and to reveal all their potential qualities, in order to create the conditions necessary for their "fusion into a single common culture and common language." And to explain this contradiction, he resorts to another equally apparent contradiction, possibly on the assumption that one incongruity would resolve the other. "Aren't we," Stalin asks, "for the 'withering away' of the state, but at the same time in favor of the strengthening of the dictatorship of the proletariat which represents the most powerful and mighty of all forms of state power that have hitherto existed?" Development of national culture, in spite of the ultimate cosmopolitan goal, is held to be as little contradictory as development of state power in spite of the ultimate "withering away" of the state, both apparent contradictions being rooted and, according to Stalin, resolving themselves in Marxian dialectics.

No doubt, Stalin believed that Lenin had espoused the idea of the ultimate fusion of national cultures and languages and the disappearance of ethnic units. At the same time he is unequivocally opposed to embarking on the road to cosmopolitanism at the time of his discussion of the nationality problem (1925, 1930) and denounces those who are ready to set out on this journey as "Great Russian Chauvinists." While implying that the Party will take this road some time in the distant future, he holds that at present the accepted route is the one leading to the development of national culture; this is in a direction opposite to that claimed to be ultimately unavoidable and from the Communist standpoint also desirable, namely the fusion of different ethnic units and their cultures and languages.

The question may be raised whether Stalin did not pay mere lip service to the ultimate amalgamation of nations, in view especially of the well known nationality policy of the Soviet Union which helped develop national languages and cultures, even of the less advanced and backward peoples. This appears to be most likely. It is borne out by a talk of Stalin in 1925 when he attributed the goal of a "single universal language in the period of socialism and dying away of all other languages" not to Lenin, the revered teacher, but to Karl Kautsky, the arch-villain himself, and added: "I have little faith in this theory of a single, all-embracing language" (*ibid.*, 196). It would appear that this position of Stalin, then very much in line with Soviet national and cultural policy, expresses better and more accurately his real views in this matter.—See also Stalin's rejection in 1921 of the charge that "we Communists are cultivating artificially" the White Russian and Ukrainian nationalities. The latter existed, he maintained, "and it is the duty of Communists to develop [!] their culture. We must not go counter to history" (109-10). In the same year he also remarked: "We must save the Kirghiz and Bashkirs from extinction" (103) and "Proletarian in content, national in form—such is the universal human culture towards which socialism is marching" (195); E. H. Carr, *op. cit.,* I, 377, holds that if any criticism of the Soviet Government is to be made on the point of fostering the cultural development of non-Russian nationalities, "it is perhaps that it went too far in encouraging the resuscitation of primitive or half-decayed languages and cultures."

15. "The Socialist Revolution (. . .)," *Soch.,* XIX, 40; italics Lenin's.

16. *Ibid.*

17. *Ibid.;* see also "Discussion (. . .)," *Soch.,* XIX, 245, where the proletariat is directed to "plead for unity, for amalgamation into an international community."

18. "The Revolutionary Proletariat (. . .)," *Soch.,* XVIII, 328; see also H. Kohn, *Nationalism in the Soviet Union,* p. 47, where the author speaks of "territorial amalgamation" and remarks: "With the achievement of socialism, nationalism will gradually disappear and the nationality question will steadily lose importance."

Cf. also Avrahm Yarmolinsky, *The Jews and other Minor Nationalities under the Soviets* (N. Y., 1928), p. 9: "Nothing seemed to him [Lenin] more desirable than the obliteration of political frontiers and the merging of peoples." That the disappearance of nationalities was expected by Lenin is also the view of J. Towster, *Political Power in the Soviet Union* . . .: "Ultimately, there would be no nationalism of any kind" (54). While, in general, this view is no doubt correct, it must be said that Lenin has not been too explicit about this matter, and that it is not always clear whether his references to "merger," "amalgamation," etc. have political or ethnic significance, or both.

NOTES FOR CONCLUSION

1.   "The Socialist Revolution (. . .)," *Soch.*, XIX, 40.

2.   "The Cadets and the 'Self-Determination of the Nations,' " *Soch.*, XVII, 109.

3.   Lenin was sharply critical of the Left which maintained: " 'The right to self-determination is not applicable to socialist society.' " ("Discussion [. . .]," *Soch.*, XIX, 242); see also "A Caricature (. . .)," *Soch.*, XIX, 220.

4.   It is revealing that Lenin, in spite of his frequent discussions of the nationality question in general, avoids referring to this resolution.

5.   Writing in Germany in 1941, Werner von Harpe, *Die Grundsaetze der Nationalitaetenpolitik Lenin's* (the essay was not to be read by the German public, but was "nur fuer den Dienstgebrauch") noticed correctly that in some respects Lenin, theoretically, seemed to "approve" nationality, while in others he seemed to turn against the right of existence of "genuine nationality" (74); yet he maintained naively that the contradiction "dissolved" itself, if one looked on Lenin's views from the viewpoint of the materialist conception of history (85). Lenin's contradiction can not be "solved" from the viewpoint of Marxism, but is understandable if seen against the background of the exigencies of political and tactical flexibility; about the importance of "flexibility," of opportunism, for Lenin's thinking in general, see H. B. Mayo, *Democracy and Marxism* (N. Y., 1955), p. 91.

NOTES FOR CHAPTER SEVEN

1. *Soch.,* XVII, 12-13.

2. *Pervyi Vserossüsskii S'ezd Sovetov Robochikh, Soldatskikh i Krestianskikh Deputatov* (Moscow-Leningrad, 1931), II, 168.

3. *Vtoroi Vserossisskii S'ezd Sovetov* (. . .) (Moscow-Leningrad, 1928), held Nov. 7-8, 1917, p. 9.

4. Frank Lorimer, *The Population of the Soviet Union. History and Prospects* (Geneva, 1946), pp. 39f.

5. Quoted by W. Kolarz, *Russia and her Colonies* (N. Y., 1945), p. 7.

6. *Sobranie Uzakonenii.* 1917-18, No. 2 (2nd ed.), art. 18; quoted by Carr, *op. cit.,* I, 263.

7. Kliuchnikov i Sabanin, *Mezhdunarodnaia Politika,* II (1926), 94-96.

8. *Tretii Vserossiskii S'ezd Sovetov* (1918), pp. 77-80.

9. E. H. Carr, *op. cit.,* I, 267.

10. *VKP(B),* (1941), I, 286-87.

11. B. Souvarine, *Stalin* (N. Y., 1939), maintains: "The squaring of the nationality circle was insoluble without belying theory in practice" (201), but briefly admits in another connection that "Lenin's doctrine of nationality," far from being consistent, was "hesitant, confused and contradictory" (200).

12. For a thorough account and evaluation of the history of "Self-Determination in Practice," see E. H. Carr, *The Bolshevik Revolution,* I, chaps. 11 and 12, also 10, 13, and 14, and R. Pipes, *The Formation of the Soviet Union* (Cambridge, 1954).

13. About the varied history of Georgia after the October Revolution, see R. Pipes, *op. cit.,* chap. v; especially pp. 235-36 and 239-40, about Lenin's opposition first to the invasion of Georgia—which was advocated by Stalin and Ordzonikidze and carried out by them without Lenin's knowledge in the spring of 1921—his later reconciliation with it, and his warnings against applying rough-and-ready methods of government in formerly Menshevik-dominated Georgia; see also Carr, *op. cit.,* I, 394-97.

14. *Izvestiia,* Jan. 21, 1937, quoted by R. Pipes, *op. cit.,* p. 272.

15. Note of December 31, 1922; quoted by R. Pipes, *op. cit.,* p. 276. This is one of three letters quoted in the following and translated by R. Pipes, pp. 273-77, from a copy made by Trotsky and now in the Harvard College Library, Trotsky Archive; the letters were originally not written for publication.

16.   *Ibid.* See for the following also Trotsky, L. *The Stalin School of Falsification* (N. Y., 1937), esp. pp. 65-71: Lenin's Letters on the National Question.

17.   *Ibid.*, p. 75.

18.   See also Lenin's letters of March, 1923, quoted by Wolfe, *op. cit.*, pp. 426 f., espec. 446-47; also Trotsky, *op. cit.*, pp. 69-70.

19.   This disagreement was after 1917 not as wide as in 1913, but nevertheless in existence. Lenin, his eyes always on political and ethnic amalgamation, changed his views after the Revolution, but never became enthusiastic about fostering national cultures.

20.   Stalin, *Marxism and the National and Colonial Question* (N. Y., 1942).

21.   Lenin's letter of Dec. 30, 1922, quoted by R. Pipes, *op. cit.*, p. 274.

22.   B. D. Wolfe, *op. cit.*, p. 404.

23.   Lenin's letter of Dec. 30, 1922, quoted by Pipes, *op. cit.*, p. 273.

24.   *Ibid.*, p. 274; Dec. 30 and 31, 1922.

25.   *Ibid.*

26.   *Ibid.*, pp. 274-75; Dec. 31, II., Cont. of Notes.

27.   *Ibid.*, pp. 275-76; Dec. 31.

28.   *Ibid.*, p. 274, Dec. 30.

29.   See especially his *State and Revolution.*

30.   Lenin's letter of Dec. 31; quoted by Pipes, *op. cit.*, p. 277.

31.   Letter of Dec. 31, *ibid.*, p. 275.

Bibliography

Chapter I

Documentary and other Primary Sources

Begeulov, A., ed., *Leninizm i Natsional'nyi Vopros* (Rostov on the Don, 1931) (Leninism and the Nationality Question); contains some speeches and letters of Lenin and other diverse material on the national problem, but inadequate in regard to Lenin's position on nationality.

International Socialist Congress at Stuttgart, Aug. 18-24, 1907 (Berlin, 1907).

International Socialist Workers and Trade Union Congress (London, 1896); see also the German version: *Verhandlungen und Beschluesse des Internationalen Arbeiter-und Gewerkschaftskongresses zu London* (Berlin, 1897).

Lenin, V. I., *Sochineniia* (Moscow, 1926-32), Second Ed., 30 vols. (Collected Works).

Velikovskii, M. and Lenin, I., eds., *Natsional'nyi Vopros, Chrestomatiia* (Moscow, 1931) (The Nationality Problem, An Anthology); contains brief essays and selections, with short introductory notes by the editors, from the pertinent works of Marx, Engels, O. Bauer, K. Renner. K. Kautsky, Bebel, Cunow, Folmer, Lensch, Pernerstorfer, Lenin, Stalin, Bukharin, Medem, G. Safarov, Piatakov; Resolutions of the Second International on the national and colonial question, etc.; a most valuable collection.

Verhandlungen des Gesamtparteitages der Sozialdemokratie in Oesterreich (Bruenn) (Vienna, 1899).

VKP (B) v Rezoliutsiiakh i Resheniakh S'ezdov (1953). (The All-Union Communist Party [B] in Resolutions and Decisions of Congresses.)

Monographs

Bauer, O. *Die Nationalitaetenfrage und die Sozialdemokratie in Marxstudien,* II (Vienna, 1924); this work appeared first in 1907; indispensable.

———— *Die Oesterreichische Revolution* (Vienna, 1923); see especially the introductory chapters.

Berlin, I. *Karl Marx, His Life and Environment* (London, 1948).

Bloom, S. F., *The World of Nations. A Study of the National Implications in the Work of Karl Marx* (New York, 1941).

Carr, E. H. *The Bolshevik Revolution 1917-23,* vol. I (New York, 1951); see pp. 410-18 on the nineteenth century background of the Bolshevik doctrine of self-determination; basic.

Cunow, H. *Die Marx'sche Geschichts-, Gesellschafts-, und Staatstheorie,* 2 vols. (Berlin, 1920-21); on nationality, see II, 9-49.

De Man, H. *Au delà du Marxisme* (Paris, 1929); see especially chap. x: "Le socialisme dans l'éspace. Du cosmopolitanisme au social patriotisme."

Deutsch, K. W. *Nationalism and Social Communication* (New York, 1953).

Encyclopedia Judaica (Berlin, 1928 f.); on the Bund, see IV, 1208.

Froelich, P. *Rosa Luxemburg. Her Life and Work.* Transl. E. Fitzgerald (London, 1940); see chap. v, pp. 36-49: The National Question as a Strategic Problem.

Hayes, C. J. H. *The Historical Evolution of Modern Nationalism* (New York, 1931).

Jászi, O. *The Dissolution of the Habsburg Monarchy* (Chicago, 1929).

Kann, R. A. *The Multinational Empire. Nationalism and National Reform in the Habsburg Monarchy 1848-1918* (New York, 1950), 2 vols.

Kastelianskii, A. I., ed. *Formy Natsional'nogo Dvizheniia v Sovremennykh Gosudarstvakh* (St. Petersburg, 1910) (Forms of the National Movement in Modern States).

Kautsky, K., *Sozialismus und Kolonialpolitik* (Berlin, 1907).

Kohn, H. *Nationalism. Its Meaning and History* (Princeton, 1955).

Le Parti Socialist-Révolutionnaire et le problème des nationalités en Russie (Paris, 1919).

Martov, J. *Geschichte der russischen Sozial-Demokratie.* Mit einem Nachwort von Th. Dan: Die Sozial-Demokratie Russlands nach dem Jahre 1908. Autorisierte Uebersetzung von A. Stein (Berlin, 1926).

Marx, K. and Engels, F. *Manifest der kommunistischen Partei* in *Marx-Engels Gesamtausgabe,* ed. V. Adoratskii, I Abt., vol. 6.

———— *Gesammelte Schriften,* ed. F. Mehring (Stuttgart, 1902); vol. III contains numerous articles on the nationality question.

———— *Revolution and Counter-Revolution in Germany in 1848,* ed. Eleanor Marx-Aveling (London, 1896).

Masaryk, Th. G. *Die philosophischen und soziologischen Grundlagen des Marxismus* (Vienna, 1899); see especially pp. 426 ff.: "Nationalitaet und Internationalitaet."

Medem, Z. B. W. *Sotsialdemokratiia i Natsional'nyi Vopros* (St. Petersburg, 1901) (Social Democracy and the National Question).

Mehring, F. "Die polnische Frage," *Nachlass* (Berlin, 1924), III, 18-44.

Minski, E. L., ed. *The National Question in the Russian Duma* (London, 1915).

Pipes, R. *The Formation of the Soviet Union 1917-23* (Cambridge, 1954). Thorough; has also an excellent bibliography on the Russian nationality problem.

Rafes, M. *Ocherki po Istorii "Bunda"* (Moscow, 1923) (Essays on the History of the Bund).

Ravich-Cherkasskii, M., ed. *Marksizm i Natsional'nyi Vopros* (Kharkov, 1923) (Marxism and the National Question).

Renner, K. *Der Kampf der oesterreichischen Nationen um den Staat* (Vienna, 1902), Part 1.

———— *Grundlagen und Entwicklungsziele der oesterreichisch-ungarischen Monarchie* (Vienna, 1906).

————— *Das Selbstbestimmungsrecht der Nationen in beson-derer Anwendung auf Oesterreich* (completely revised edition of his earlier work: *Der Kampf der oesterreichischen Nationen*).

Wolfe, B. D. *Three Who Made a Revolution* (N. Y., 1948); on Marx and the nationality question, see pp. 568-77.

Zhitlovsky, Ch. "Der Sozialismus und die nationale Frage," *Gesammelte Schriften,* vol. XIII (Warsaw, 1935).

Zinoviev, G. E. *Istoriia Rossiiskoi Kommunisticheskoi Partii* (Moscow, 1923) (History of the Russian Communist Party).

Periodicals

Cunow, H. "Marx und das Selbstbestimmungsrecht der Nationen," *Die Neue Zeit,* XXXVI, 577-84.

Kautsky, K. "Finis Poloniae?" *Die Neue Zeit,* XIV, pt. 2 (1895-96), 484-91.

————— "Nationalitaet und Internationalitaet," *Die Neue Zeit,* Ergaenzungsheft No. 1 (Stuttgart, 1908).

Luxemburg, R. "Die neuen Stroemungen in der polnischen sozialistischen Bewegung in Deutschland und Oesterreich," *Die Neue Zeit,* Nos. 32 and 33, 1896.

————— "Der Sozialpatriotismus in Polen," *Die Neue Zeit,* No. 41, 1896.

Riazanov, D. "Karl Marx und Friedrich Engels ueber die Polenfrage," *Archiv fuer die Geschichte des Sozialismus und der Arbeiterbewegung,* VI, 175-221.

Velikovsky, A. "Marx i Engels o natsional'nom voprose" (Marx and Engels on the National Question), *Sovetskoe Gosu-darstvo,* No. 3 (1933), pp. 43-51.

Chapters II-VI

(Most of the sources listed under chapter I which pertain also to the following chapters are not repeated here.)

Primary Sources

Begeulov, A., ed. *Leninizm i Natsional'nyi Vopros* (Rostov on the Don, 1931) (Leninism and the National Question).

Hille, E. and Mudie, D., ed. and transl. *The Letters of Lenin* (New York, 1953).

Lenin, V. I. *Sochineniia* (Moscow, 1926-32), Second ed., 30 vols. (Collected Works).

No attempt is here made to list all of Lenin's writings which, directly or indirectly, deal with the nationality question, though his important essays and articles on this topic have been included in the following. The most valuable guide to Lenin's writings is the Subject Index to the second and third editions of Lenin's *Sochineniia,* namely *Predmetnyi ukazatel' ko II i III izdaniiam sochinenii Lenina,* 1934. For Lenin's drafts and other notes, see *Leninskii sbornik.*

Lenin, V. I. "Chto takoe druz'ia naroda?" (Who Are the Friends of the People?), *Soch.,* I, 55-222 (written in April, 1894).

———— "Proekt i obiasnenie programmy s.-d. partii" (Draft and Explanation of the Program of the Social Democratic Party), *Soch.,* I, 425-45 (written 1895-96).

———— "Zadachi russkikh' sotsial demokratov" (The Tasks of Russian Social Democrats), *Soch.,* II, 171-87.

———— "Kitaiska voina" (The Chinese War), *Soch.,* IV, 60-64.

———— "K voprosu o programme" (On the Problem of the Program), *Soch.,* IV. 174-81 (written in Sept., 1902).

———— "O manifeste armianskikh sotsial demokratov" (The Manifest of the Armenian Social Democrats), *Soch.,* V, 241-44.

———— "Protest finlandskogo naroda" (The Protest of the Finnish People), *Soch.,* IV, 335-38.

———— "Pro povodu zaiavleniia bunda" (At the Occasion of the Declaration of the Bund).

———— "Nuzhna li 'samostoiatel'naia politicheskaia partiia' evreiskomu proletariatu?" (Does the Jewish proletariat need an 'independent political Party' "?), *Soch.,* V, 245-49.

———— "Natsional'nyi vopros v nashei programme" (The National Question in Our Program), *Soch.,* V, 337-44.

————— "Proekt rezoliutsii o meste bunda v partii" (Project of a Resolution on the Place of the Bund in the Party), *Soch.,* VI, 6.

————— "Rech' po voprosu o meste bunda v partii" (Talk on the Question of the Position of the Bund in the Party), *Soch.,* VI, 18-20.

————— "Pervaia rech' po voprosu o poriadke dnia s'ezda 31 July" (First Speech on the Question of the Agenda of the Party Congress, July, 31), *Soch.,* VI, 14.

————— "Polozhenie bunda v partii" (The Position of the Bund in the Party), *Soch.,* VI, 78-86.

————— "K evreiskim rabochim" (To the Jewish Workers), *Soch.,* VIII, 24-26.

————— "O 'natsional'nykh' s.-d. organizatsiiakh" (On 'National' Social Democratic Organizations), *Soch.,* XVI, 234-35.

————— "Separatisty v Rossii i separatisty v Avstrii" (Separatists in Russia and Separatists in Austria), *Soch.,* XVI, 385-86.

————— "Rabochii klass i natsional'nyi vopros" (The Working Class and the National Question), *Soch.,* XVI, 389-90.

————— "Tezisy po natsional'nomu voprosu" (Theses on the National Question), *Soch.,* XVI, 507-13.

————— "Natsionalizatsiia evreiskoi shkoly" (Nationalization of the Jewish School), *Soch.,* XVI, 553-54.

————— "Liberaly i demokraty v voprose o iazykakh" (Liberals and Democrats on the Question of Languages), *Soch.,* XVI, 595-97.

————— "O Chernosotenstve" (On the Black-Hundred), *Soch.,* XVI, 641-42.

————— "Rezoliutsiia po natsional'nomu voprosu. Rezoliutsiia letnego 1913 goda soveshchaniia Ts. K. R. S.-D. R. P. s partiinymi rabotnikami" (Resolution On the National Question. Resolution of the Summer Conference of 1913 of the Central Committee of the R. S. D. W. P. with Party Workers), *Soch.,* XVII, 11-13.

————— "Platforma k IV s'ezdu sotsial-demokratii latyshskogo kraia" (Platform for the Fourth Party Congress of the

Social Democracy of the Latvian Region), *Soch.*, XVII, 61-67.

———— "Pis'mo S. G. Shaumianu" (Letter to Shaumian), *Soch.*, XVII, 89-91.

———— "O 'kulturno-natsional'noi' avtonomii" (On 'Cultural-National' Autonomy), *Soch.*, XVII, 92-95.

———— "Natsional'nyi sostav uchashchikhsia v russkoi shkole" (The National Affiliation of Students in the Russian School), *Soch.*, XVII, 113-15.

———— "O natsional'noi programme R. S.-D. R. P." (About the National Program of the R. S. D. W. P.), *Soch.*, XVII, 116-21

———— "Eshche o razdelenii shkol'nogo dela po natsional'nostiam" (More on Separation of Schooling According to Nationalities), *Soch.*, XVII, 124-26.

———— "Kriticheskie zametki po natsional'nomu voprosu" (Critical Notes on the National Question), *Soch.*, XVII, 129-59. This essay was first published in the Bolshevik journal *Prosveshcheniie,* October and December, 1913.

———— "Natsional-liberalizm i pravo natsii na samoopredelenie" (National-Liberalism and the Right of Nations to Self-Determination), *Soch.*, XVII, 168-69.

———— " 'Novoe Vremia' i 'rech" o prave samoopredeleniia natsii" ('New Time' and the 'Speech' on the Right to National Self-Determination), *Soch.*, XVII, 175-76.

———— "Nuzhen li obiazatel'nyi gosudarstvennyi iazyk?" (Is it necessary to establish a State Language?), *Soch.*, XVII, 179-81.

———— "K istorii natsional'noi programmy v Avstrii i v Rossii" (Toward a History of the National Program in Austria and Russia), *Soch.*, XVII, 202-204.

———— "Eshche o 'natsionalizme' " (More on 'Nationalism'), *Soch.*, XVII, 219-20.

———— "Natsional'noe ravnopravie" (National Equality), *Soch.*, XVII, 321-22.

———— "K voprosu o natsional'noi politike" (On the Question of National Policy), *Soch.*, XVII, 323-29.

————— "O prave natsii na samoopredelenie" (On the Right of Nations to Self-Determination), *Soch.*, XVII, 425-74; this essay was originally published in the Party magazine *Prosveshcheniie*, Nos. 4 and 6, 1914.

————— "O natsional'noi gordosti velikorossov" (On the National Pride of the Great Russians), *Soch.*, XVIII, 80-83.

————— "Sotsializm i voina" (Socialism and War. Attitude of the R. S. D. R. P. towards the War), *Soch.*, XVIII, 185-223.

————— "Revoliutsionnyi proletariat i pravo natsii na samoopredelenie" (The Revolutionary Proletariat and the Right of Nations to Self-Determination), *Soch.*, XVIII, 323-28.

————— "Sotsialisticheskaia revoliutsiia i pravo natsii na samoopredelenie. Tezisy" (The Socialist Revolution and the Right of Nations to Self-Determination. Theses), *Soch.*, XIX, 37-48. The theses, first published in the *Vorbote*, the theoretical organ of the Zimmerwald Left (No. 2, April, 1916), were designed to repudiate the views of the Polish Zimmerwald Left (Radek) and of the followers of Bukharin who opposed the Bolshevik slogan of national self-determination.

————— "O germanskom i ne germanskom shovinizme" (On German and non-German Chauvinism), *Soch.*, XIX, 64-66.

————— "Imperializm, kak vysshaia stadiia kapitalizma" (Imperialism, the Highest Stage of Capitalism), *Soch.*, XIX, 67-175.

————— "O broshiure Juniusa" (On the Junius Brochure), *Soch.*, XIX, 176-190.

————— "O karikature na marksizma i ob 'imperialisticheskom ekonomizme' " (A Caricature of Marxism and 'Imperialist Economism'), *Soch.*, XIX, 191-235.

————— "Pis'mo N. D. Kiknadze" (Letter to N. D. Kiknadze), *Soch.*, XIX, 236.

————— "Itogi diskussii o samoopredelenii" (Results of the Discussion on Self-Determination), *Soch.*, XIX, 239-272.

————— "Proekt pererabotki programmy" (Projected Revision of the Party Program), written in May, 1917, *Soch.*, XX, 295.

————— "Ukraina" (The Ukraine), *Soch.,* XX, 2, 534-35.

————— "Ukraina i porazhenie praviashchikh partii rossii" (The Ukraine and the Defeat of the Russian Government Parties), *Soch.,* XX, 2, 539-41.

————— "Dopolnitel'nye tezisy po natsional'nomu i kolonial'-nomu voprosam" (Additions to the Theses on the National and Colonial Question), XXV, 573-75.

Monographs

Beria, L. *On the History of the Bolshevik Organizations in Transcaucasia* (Moscow, 1949); see especially chap. iv.

Broido, G. I. *Natsional'nyi i Kolonial'nyi Vopros* (The National and Colonial Question) (Moscow, 1924).

Deutscher, I. *Stalin. A Political Biography* (London, 1949).

Fainsod, M. *How Russia Is Ruled* (Cambridge, 1953); see especially chap. xi: Constitutional Myths and Political Realities.

Harpe, W. von *Die Grundsaetze der Nationalitaetenpolitik Lenin's* (Berlin, 1941); on Lenin's thought on nationality, see pp. 74-93.

Harper, S. N. and Thompson, R. *The Government of the Soviet Union.* Secd Ed. (New York, 1949).

Hill, Chr. *Lenin and the Russian Revolution* (London, 1947); see especially chap. vi: Small Nations and Great Powers.

Janovsky, O. I. *Nationalities and National Minorities.* With Special Reference to East- and Central Europe (New York, 1945); see especially chap. vi.

Knorin, W., ed. *History of the Communist Party of the Soviet Union. A Short History.* (Moscow-Leningrad, 1935).

Kohn, H. *Nationalism in the Soviet Union* (New York, 1933); on Lenin's thought on nationality, see pp. 43-48.

Lamont, C. *Peoples of the Soviet Union* (New York, 1934).

Low, A. D. *Austria Between Two Soviet Republics. In the Mirror of the Russian Press of 1919* (unpublished essay, The Russian Institute, Columbia University, 1956); see especially "The Comintern on the International Situation," pp. 45-58 and 88-92.

Maynard, J. *Russia in Flux* (New York, 1951); see especially chaps. xxiii: The Background of the Nationalities: Unity and Disunity, and xxiv, on Soviet nationality policy.

Mayo, H. B. *Democracy and Marxism* (New York, 1955).

Miliukov, P. N. *Natsional'nyi Vopros* (Prague, 1925) (The Nationality Question); see especially the last chapter. On Lenin, see pp. 183-84.

Nationalism. A Report by a Study Group of Members of the Royal Institute of International Affairs (London, 1939); see chap. v: The Rise of Russian Nationalism. On Lenin, see pp. 72-75.

Popov, N. N. *Lenin o Natsional'nom Voprose* (Moscow, 1924) (Lenin on the National Question).

Sabine, G. H. *A History of Political Theory.* Rev. Ed. (New York, 1950).

Safarov, G. *Natsional'nyi Vopros i Proletariat* (Petrograd, 1922) (The National Question and the Proletariat); on Lenin, see pp. 115-120 and 132-38.

Schlesinger, R. *Federalism in Central and Eastern Europe* (London, 1945); especially chaps. ix and xiii.

Sorin, I. "Vladimir Ilyich Lenin," in Lenin, *Selected Works,* I.

Souvarine, B. *Stalin* (New York, 1939).

Stalin, J. "Marksizm i natsional'nyi vopros" (Marxism and the National Question), in *Sochineniia,* II (Moscow, 1946).

————— *Marxism and the National and Colonial Question* (New York, 1942).

————— *Voprosy Leninizma* (Problems of Leninism), 11th ed. (Moscow, 1947); see especially "The Foundations of Leninism," pp. 45 f.

Towster, J. *Political Power in the U. S. S. R. 1917-47* (New York, 1948); chaps. iv and v deal with the nationality problem; on Lenin's pertinent political thought see especially pp. 50-62, 80-81, and 93-94.

Trotsky, L. *The History of the Russian Revolution* (New York, 1932), 3 vols.

————— *Stalin* (New York, 1941).

Vyshinsky, A. Y. *The Law of the Soviet State* (New York, 1948), transl. by H. W. Babb.

Webb, S. and B. *Soviet Communism: A New Civilization,* Third Ed. (London, 1947).

Wilson, E. *To the Finland Station* (New York, 1953).

Wolfe, B. D. *Three Who Made a Revolution* (New York, 1948); see especially chap. xxxiii.

Yarmolinsky, A. *The Jews and Other Minor Nationalities Under the Soviets* (New York, 1928).

Periodicals and Journals

Baevskii, D. "Bol'sheviki v bor'be za III Internatsional" (The Bolsheviks in the Struggle for the Third International), *Istorik Marksist,* XI (1929), 12-48; on Lenin, especially pp. 35 f.

Khodorov, A. E. "Lenin i natsional'nyi vopros" (Lenin and the National Question), *Novyi Vostok,* No. 5, 1924, 14-43.

Page, St. W. "Lenin, the National Question, and the Baltic States 1917-19," *The American Slavic and East European Review,* Feb. 1948, No. 1.

Pavlovich, M. "Lenin i natsional'nyi vopros" (Lenin and the National Question), *Pod Znamenem Marksizma,* I (1924), 164-88; on Lenin especially p. 175 f.

Radek, K. "Das Selbstbestimmungsrecht der Voelker," *Licht-strahlen,* Berlin, No. 3, Dec. 5, 1915.

———— "Annexionen und Sozialdemokratie. Der sozial-demokratische Standpunkt," *Berner Tagwacht,* No. 252 and 253, Oct. 28 and 29, 1916.

Trainin, I. (Nation and Multinational State in the Works of Comrade Stalin), *Sovetskoe Gosudarstvo i Pravo,* No. 6 (1939), pp. 25-47.

Chapter VII

(Sources, books, and articles previously listed and pertaining also to this chapter are not repeated in the following.)

Sources

Degras, J. ed. *Soviet Documents on Foreign Policy. 1917-1924* (London, 1951) vol. I.

Dimanshtein, S. M., ed. *Revoliutsiia i Natsional'nyi Vopros* (Moscow) (The Revolution and the National Question), vol. III; a most valuable source book for the history of the nationality problem in Russia in 1917.

Kun, B., ed. *Kommunisticheskii Internatsional v Dokumentakh 1919-32* (Moscow, 1933) (The Communist International in Documents 1919-32).

Pervyi Vserossiiskii S'ezd Sovetov (Moscow-Leningrad, 1931) (First All-Russian Congress of Soviets).

Vtoroi Vserossiiskii S'ezd Sovetov (Moscow-Leningrad, 1928) (Second All-Russian Congress of Soviets).

Monographs

Barghoorn, Chs. *Soviet Russian Nationalism* (New York, 1956).

Batsell, W. R. *Soviet Rule in Russia* (New York, 1929); see especially chaps. III and X.

Bauer, R. A., Inkeles, A. and Kluckhohn, C. *How the Soviet System Works* (Cambridge, 1956); see especially "Nationality Groups," pp. 199-208.

Caroe, O. *Soviet Empire, the Turks of Central Asia, and Stalin* (London, 1953).

Chernov, F. *Proletarskii Internatsionalizm i Burzhuaznyi Kospolitizm* (Moscow, 1951) (Proletarian Internationalism and Bourgeois Cosmopolitanism).

Chernov, V. *The Great Russian Revolution* (New Haven, 1936); see particularly chap. xiv.

Chesnokov, D. I. "Marksizm-Leninizm ob otechestve i patriotizme" (Marxism-Leninism on Fatherland and Patriotism) in *O sovetskom Patriotizme,* rev. ed. (Moscow, 1952) (On Soviet Patriotism).

Inodoretz, *La Russie et les peuples allogènes* (Berne, 1917).

Haumant, E. *Le Problème de l'unité Russe* (Paris, 1922).

Kolarz, W. *Russia and her Colonies* (London, 1952).

Kovalev, S. *O Natsional'noi Gordosti Sovietskikh Lyudei* (Moscow, 1950) (On the National Pride of Soviet People).

Kulski, W. W. *The Soviet Regime* (Syracuse, 1954); see especially pp. 1-129 and 742-46.

Lorimer, F. *The Population of the Soviet Union. History and Prospects* (Geneva, 1946).

Mainardi, L. *U. S. S. R. prigione di popoli* (Rome, 1941).

Popov, N. N. *Oktiabr'skaia Revoliutsiia i Natsional'nyi Vopros* (Moscow, 1923) (The October Revolution and the National Question).

Rysakoff, A. *The National Policy of the Soviet Union* (London, 1931).

Schwarz, S. M. *The Jews in the Soviet Union* (Syracuse, 1951).

Smal-Stocki, R. *The Nationality Problem of the Soviet Union* (Milwaukee, 1952).

Strong, A. L. *Peoples of the U. S. S. R.* (New York, 1944); especially pp. 58-68.

Timoshenko, V. P. "Soviet Agricultural Policy and the Nationalities Problem in the U. S. S. R." in *Report on the Soviet Union in 1956*. A Symposium of the Institute for the Study of the U. S. S. R. (New York, 1956), pp. 31-50.

Trotsky, L. *The Stalin School of Falsification* (New York, 1937); see Letters on the National Question, pp. 65-71.

Periodicals

Aziyan, A. "Razvitie tovarishchem Stalinym marksistsko-leninskoi teorii po natsional'nomu voprosu" *Bol'shevik* (Feb. 1950), No. 3, pp. 21-36 (The Development of the Marxist-Leninist Theory on the Nationality Question by Comrade Stalin).

Barghoorn, F. Chs. "Nationality Doctrine in Soviet Political Strategy," *The Review of Politics* (July, 1954), vol. No. 3, pp. 283-304.

Biehahn, W. "Marxismus und die nationale Idee in Russland," *Osteuropa*, IX (1933-1934), pp. 461-76.

Chamberlin, W. H. "Soviet Race and Nationality Policies," *Russian Review*, V, No. 1 (1945), pp. 3-9.

Eudin, X. "Soviet National Minority Policies, 1918-21," *The Slavonic and East European Review,* XXI (1943), pt. 2, 31-55.

Goldstein, A. "The Soviet Attitude Towards Territorial Minorities and the Jews," publ. by the Institute of Jewish Affairs (New York, 1953).

Kurganov, I. "The Problem of Nationalities in Soviet Russia," *Russian Review,* Oct. 1951, pp. 253-67.

Reshetar, J. S., Jr. "National Deviation in the Soviet Union," *The American Slavic and East European Review,* vol. XII (Apr. 1953).

Semenoff, G. "Die Nationale Frage in der Russischen Revolution," *Zeitschrift fuer Politik,* XIV (1924-25).

Stalin, J. "Oktiabr'skaia revoliutsiia i natsional'naia politika russkikh kommunistov" (The October Revolution and the Nationality Policy of the Russian Communists), *Pravda,* Nov. 6-7, 1921; see also *Sochineniia* (1946-   ), V, 113-16.

Index

191